MLIWK

To Mue

Books are to be returned on
the la...

with best wishes

Peter Hennor

NEW DEALS

"This is a highly readable, action-packed book, which would be essential reading for human resource professionals and managers interested in the revolution, which is about to overtake us all in the nature of managerial careers and corporate life."

Cary L. Cooper
Professor of Organizational Psychology, UMIST, UK

"This is a refreshing, no-nonsense, down to earth study of what is really happening in organisational restructuring. The authors get underneath the hype, jargon and double speak which have characterised the recent years of "transformation", and take the individual's perspective. The good news is that they are not content with merely a researcher's description of their findings, but they devote the second half of the book to a guide to renegotiating personal change. You don't have to lie back and take it all ..."

Andrew Mayo
Director of People Development, ICL plc, UK

*"***New Deals** *goes beyond defining the problems caused by workforce redundancies.* It specifically outlines the new employment contract necessary for both individual and organizational survival. A very important book and a must-read for organizational leaders."

David Noer
Center for Creative Leadership, North Carolina, USA

"The analysis offered in **New Deals** *is excellent,* and a good analysis is 90 per cent of the way towards a solution. We all need to address the issues raised in this book as an urgent priority—we've got to stop using people as machines before it's too late."

Christopher Haskins
Chairman, Northern Foods, UK

"Everyone knows that the managerial career is changing radically: this excellent, admirably concise book not only shows how and why, but most convincingly tells managers—as both employers and employees—what fundamental and practical changes must be made to avert organisational and personal crisis."

Robert Heller
Author of Naked Manager for the 90's

NEW DEALS

The Revolution in Managerial Careers

PETER HERRIOT

CAROLE PEMBERTON

JOHN WILEY & SONS
Chichester ✦ New York ✦ Brisbane ✦ Toronto ✦ Singapore

Other Wiley Editorial Offices

John Wiley & Sons, Inc., 605 Third Avenue,
New York, NY 10158-0012, USA

Jacaranda Wiley Ltd, 33 Park Road, Milton,
Queensland 4064, Australia

John Wiley & Sons (Canada) Ltd, 22 Worcester Road,
Rexdale, Ontario M9W 1L1, Canada

John Wiley & Sons (SEA) Pte Ltd, 37 Jalan Pemimpin #05-04,
Block B, Union Industrial Building, Singapore 2057

Library of Congress Cataloging-in-Publication Data

Herriot, Peter.
    New deals : the revolution in managerial careers / Peter Herriot
and Carole Pemberton.
        p. cm.
    Includes bibliographical references and index.
    ISBN 0-471-95799-2
    1. Management—Vocational guidance. 2. Organizational change.
3. Deals. 4. Management—Vocational guidance—Great Britain.
5. Executives—Great Britain. I. Pemberton, Carole. II. Title.
    HD38.2.H47 1995
    658'.0023'73—dc20   95–2362
                                                              CIP

British Library Cataloguing in Publication Data

A catalogue record for this book is available from the British Library

ISBN 0-471-95799-2

Typeset in 11/13 pt Palatino from the authors' disks by Production Technology Department,
John Wiley & Sons, Chichester
Printed and bound in Great Britain by Biddles Ltd, Guildford, Surrey
This book is printed on acid-free paper responsibly manufactured from sustainable forestation, for which
at least two trees are planted for each one used for paper production.

To Jane

CONTENTS

CONTENTS

CONTENTS

PART FOUR
THE NEW SURVIVAL STRATEGY

PART FIVE
ORGANIZATIONAL CONTRACTING

CONTENTS

PART SIX
INDIVIDUAL CONTRACTING

ABOUT THE AUTHORS

Peter Herriot is Director of Research, Sundridge Park Management Centre and Visiting Professor, City University Business School. Previously he was Professor of Occupational Psychology, Birkbeck College, University of London and Professor of Psychology, City University. He is the author of *Recruitment in the 90s*, *The Career Management Challenge*, and *Down from the Ivory Tower*, editor of *Assessment and Selection in Organisations*, and co-author of *Competitive Advantage through Diversity*. In mid-1995 he will move to the Institute for Employment Studies (Brighton, UK), as Associate Director, but he remains an active member of Sundridge Park Academic Board.

Carole Pemberton is Research Consultant, Sundridge Park Management Centre. Previously she was Training Manager, London Borough of Kingston, and Careers Adviser at Brighton Polytechnic. She is co-author of *Competitive Advantage through Diversity* and a frequent contributor to the national and professional press on career issues. She is a committee member of the European Women's Management Development Network.

INTRODUCTION

In the last fifteen years the confidence of the British middle class has been eroded. All over Europe and America, too, the assurance of a secure future for individuals and their families has crumbled away. What is the cause of this catastrophic collapse? *It is the permanent loss of the traditional notion of career*.

Career and profession are the twin foundations of middle-class identities, lifestyles and status. Ask a middle-class person who they are, and they will reply in terms of their occupation or profession, or perhaps in terms of their employer: "I'm an actuary, actually", or "I'm an IBMer".

The idea of career cemented the permanence of this identity. It implied a steady and assured progression through one's working life: increasing status within the profession and the organization. A flourishing career gave status over and above the cachet which mere professional membership already conferred. Careers in professions and organizations were historically the ways in which more powerful occupational groups insulated themselves against the slings and arrows of the labour market. They were what distinguished the middle from the working classes, who had to rely on their unions for what job security they could secure for them.

So important a part of their identity is their professional career that many redundant managers cannot bring themselves to admit, either to themselves or to their nearest and dearest, that the worst has happened. Stories abound of sacked executives continuing to catch the 7.45 to the City and sitting on a park bench all day. People only engage in denial when they have lost something or someone that is profoundly important to them. What they have lost here is a large part of themselves.

Another reason for denial is the loss of the lifestyle that a solid career brings with it. The grammar school boys of the post-war settlement felt that they had earned their new style and status. They deserved it, and their parents were proud of them. These self-made men mistakenly thought that they could sit back and enjoy their own creation. Moreover, now that they had learned the ropes, they were confident that they in turn could guide their own children through the academic maze. The prize at the end was a qualification and therefore, by definition, a career. This was the middle-class equivalent of the aristocratic inheritance of stately home and family silver. What I have I hold, and I pass it on to my children.

Gone, all gone, and for ever. The futurologists' promises in the 1970s of a lifetime of professional or managerial work interspersed with leisure time and personal development were a cruel deceit. Not only did these pretensions turn out to be a mirage; so did the very basis of career itself—reliable employment with regular promotions.

The employing organizations are facing a crisis of equal magnitude, however. Organizational survival just as much as personal survival is a major challenge. Insolvencies are a matter of everyday report; acquisitions, mergers and divestments are frequent events. Deregulation and the globalization of markets have increased the level of competition organizations have to face, while the increased size and frequency of the economic cycle of boom and bust make it next to impossible to develop strategies to win.

It's hardly surprising that organizations have battened down the hatches to survive. They have sought to remain or to become cost-competitive, paying less attention to new product or service development. The need to propitiate the stock market and demonstrate short-term profitability to shareholders has encouraged them in their zeal to cut back to the bone.

This book is the story of a revolution: a revolution in the very nature of the psychological contract between managers and professionals and their organizations. We will argue that we are only halfway through this revolution. The harsh environment has caused the loss for ever of the old, long-term relational contract. This relational contract was more than just a business bargain. It implied mutual commitment and trust over the long term. It was, indeed, a relationship, the severance of which was like the break-up of many relationships—sad, painful and acrimonious.

All that's in the past, although many have still to come to terms with it. This book is about the present and the future. We want to address the following questions:

♦ What's really happening?
♦ Why is it happening?
♦ How are managers reacting?
♦ What's going to happen?
♦ How can individuals and organizations prepare for it?

The answers we came up with require new sorts of contract. They are between parties who don't automatically put the boot in if it happens to be on their foot. Hopefully, too, this book will do right by the many hundreds of our research respondents. They have shared with us their hopes, their insecurities, their feelings of injustice. Their voice needs hearing. Most of the quotations in the text are what they wrote in the open section of our research questionnaire. The remainder are from our friend Bill Manning's excellent PhD thesis, and published with his permission.

STRUCTURE OF THE BOOK

In order to help you find your way through the book's argument, and to identify the parts which are most relevant to you, the book is divided into six parts.

In Part One we look at what's been happening in organizations to cause the changes to managers' careers (Chapter One), and how Human Resources has responded to the demand to make the organization more cost-competitive (Chapter Two). In Chapter Three we outline the old career deal within which many managers' careers have been built and contrast this with the deal which is operating in 1995. In Chapter Four we look at employees' responses to what they see happening, and highlight the organizational dangers.

In Part Two, we look at why the deal has had to be changed, from the organization's perspective. In Chapters Five and Six we focus on the move to a global economy and the pressures for short-term results. In Chapters Seven and Eight we look at why organizations have accepted a number of HR fads, and critically assess whether they have made the impact that is claimed for them.

In Part Three we look at the real impact of the changes in UK organizations. In Chapter Nine we offer evidence that business changes are not necessarily assessed for their career implications by experienced managers. In Chapter Ten we focus on the feelings of inequity and injustice which employees are feeling, because of the ways in which redundancies and downsizing have been handled. We take this further in Chapters Eleven and Twelve by focusing on the feelings of powerlessness which are being experienced by many UK managers, and through identifying ways in which managers are hitting back.

In Part Four we look at new survival strategies. In Chapter Thirteen we show that it is possible for organizations to change the contract in ways which respect the human factor. In Chapter Fourteen we argue that deals of the future need to be individualized, and identify three future career deals to meet the needs of part-time workers, contract employees and core workers. We recognize difficulties in the contracting process for each of the three contracts in Chapter Fifteen. In Chapter Sixteen we draw attention to different career cultures operating in organizations, and argue the case for a new role for both HR and Trade Unions in helping the contracting process.

In Parts Five and Six we look at developing a future contracting process from the perspective of both the organization and individuals. In Chapters Seventeen to Twenty we address the need for acquiring information, negotiation, monitoring the contract and re-negotiation or exit from the perspective of the organization. In Chapters Twenty-One to Twenty-Four we look at the same stages from the perspective of the individual. For each stage we offer case studies to show theory in practice, and offer checklists to those wanting to enter negotiations.

In summary Parts One, Two and Three are intended to help those who want to gain a wider perspective on the changes that they are experiencing in their own organizations, while Parts Four, Five and Six are intended to help organizations and individuals be better equipped to contract with each other. So whether you are a pragmatist who just wants to know how to get a better deal in the future, or a theorist who wants to know why we have reached where we are, and where we may go next, this book is designed to help you make sense of a changing workplace.

Part One

WHAT'S REALLY HAPPENING?

Chapter One

THE NUMBERS GAME

PRESS PERCEPTIONS

Almost daily, the quality press drops a new bombshell onto its middle-class readers' breakfast tables. "Leaders of industry are getting a taste of their own medicine", we read[1]. A list of blue-chip companies who are making managers redundant follows: BP, BT, W. H. Smith, ICI, for example. The financial press meanwhile marvels at the "mother of all provisions"—1.6 billion set aside to restructure British Gas and shed 25,000 jobs[2]. Hand-in-hand with the redundancies go reports of a slicing in half of the managerial pyramid: from 12 down to 6 levels at BT, and from 4 down to an incredible 2 at W. H. Smith.

Managerial redundancies are often presented in the press as though they were a form of rabies. They aren't spreading up through France and threatening to cross the Channel like the real thing, however. Rather, they are seen as moving down from the industrial North, which suffered so badly in the early 1980s. The disease has now bitten into the very heartland of Thatcherism—the service sector of the fat South-East. Over 68 per cent of companies in the

South-East declared redundancies in 1991 and 1992[3]. Shipbuilding, heavy engineering, construction, mining and manufacturing suffered in the 80s. Now it's the turn of the banking, insurance, retail and leisure sectors.

The picture of an inexorable spread of redundancies across every sector of the economy is matched by another disease metaphor. The rotting away of the corporate trunk is now spreading to the flowers and fruit; while the workers suffered some time ago, those nearer the top are beginning to drop off, too. There are 3 per cent of professionals and 5 per cent of managerial, administrative and technical employees who are currently unemployed[1]. However, these categories have some more dropping off to do before they match the 7 per cent clerical, 8 per cent sales and 13 per cent craft and operatives who are unemployed.

IT'S NOT SO SIMPLE

Certainly, the media present a picture of a uniform across-the-board process of redundancy of managers and professionals which still has a long way to go. Managers themselves accept this picture—fully 88 per cent of a large and representative sample agreed that creating a slimmer and flatter organization was what they were doing to respond better to challenges and opportunities within their business environment[4]. Does the evidence as a whole support this view? Is there an overall across-the-board reduction in managers and professionals? Or is the picture more complex than this, so that we can make some informed guesses as to why downsizing and delayering are the order of the day?

A very simple first step is to uncouple downsizing and delayering from each other. They so often appear together in the press that they have become the Siamese twins of corporate restructuring. When they were separated, managers described their organization's current structure in 1992 as compared with that of 5 years before as follows[5]:

♦ Fewer managers, same levels   13%
♦ Fewer managers, fewer levels   31%

- ◆ Fewer managers, more levels   3%
- ◆ More managers, same levels   11%
- ◆ More managers, fewer levels   8%
- ◆ More managers, more levels   16%
- ◆ Unchanged   15%
- ◆ Other   3%

Here's a much more complex picture, with 35 per cent of managers actually claiming that their organizations employed *more* managers in 1992 than 5 years before. On close analysis, it appeared that it was the larger organizations which were most likely to have downsized and delayered; and it was organizations from the utilities, retail and government sectors. By contrast, professional and other services were less likely to have restructured.

To further muddy the waters, it seems that while managers and professionals are being made redundant at one end, they are being recruited at the other. And this isn't just a matter of replacing tired and expensive old stagers with keen cheap young graduates. The number of advertisements in the national press for executives has been increasing since mid- 1993[6]. The demand for managers in high technology and in retail was far higher in spring 1994 than a year previously (119 and 67 per cent respectively). In terms of function, Sales and Marketing showed the biggest increase, followed by R&D and Finance.

A top recruiter, Alan Kerby, Chairman of Moxon Dolphin Kerby, described the recruitment arena for managers in June 1994 like this: "Other than sales and marketing, middle management recruitment is probably the area that is experiencing the most significant growth at present. This is across a wide range of disciplines and functions, including human resources (particularly), engineering, manufacturing, sales and marketing of course, finance and purchasing. This seems to indicate that many companies have overdone the cutting out of so-called deadwood, and are finding that any pick-up at all in their businesses has left them deficient in many areas of middle management."

Indeed, organizations actually report skills shortages in a wide variety of areas—44 per cent in Sales and Marketing, 36 per cent in IT/Computing, and 21 per cent in Production in one local survey, for example[7].

ORGANIZATIONS IN CHANGE

So what's going on? How can both bloodletting and blood transfusion be occurring simultaneously? Consideration of the ways managers change jobs can give us some more clues.

Between 1982 and 1992, the percentage of managers who had changed their job during the course of the previous year increased from 21 to 29 per cent[8]. Managers are on the move ever more frequently, both within and between organizations. Yet there are major differences over this period in terms of the *reasons* for moving. In 1982, still in recession, 49 per cent of moves were for career development or other proactive reasons; whereas only 21 per cent were due to reorganization or otherwise enforced. By the 1992 recession, the picture was reversed. Now, 34 per cent of moves were proactive, whereas 41 per cent were enforced. Managers used to choose to move—now they are moved willy-nilly.

Some of these moves are, of course, involuntary redundancy—7 per cent in 1992 as opposed to 2 per cent ten years earlier. What's more, a higher proportion of the moves were sideways or downwards. However, many more of the job changes in 1992 are to do with other structural changes—mergers of organizations, of departments, of jobs, for example, or the creation of entirely new jobs[9]. Even in the mid-80s, half of the moves that managers made were to newly created jobs.

What, then, is the overall picture? What's really happening behind the hype? The answer is that those in power in many organizations have created structural change, usually in reaction to a perceived need to cut costs and improve productivity. The change that has gripped the attention of the media has been the one with the most obvious and immediate impact on individuals—managerial redundancies. However, this is but one of many changes; while redundancy is obviously a profoundly important one-off event, there are more gradual changes which have equally important but less obvious consequences. For example, in 1993, 89 per cent of managers reported an increase in workload and 82 per cent an increase in responsibilities[10]. No wonder 58 per cent of them work more than fifty hours a week! And no wonder that, worldwide, 85 per cent of managers are more concerned about leading a balanced life than they were five years ago[11].

Yet these are all general trends. What we need to remember also are the huge differences between organizations. Size and sector make a difference, but even within a sector one organization can manage careers totally differently from another. Amongst eight organizations in the finance sector, for example, the average length of service of middle managers in the organization in 1993 ranged from 13.9 to 26.2 years, and in present job from 3.16 to 6.18 years[12]. So organizations do adopt markedly different strategies for change. Instead of interpreting redundancy and delayering as the inevitable march of progress, we can discern several different organizational responses to the external winds of change. In the end, it is people who take the decisions, not those economic trends which trigger the need for them; and some of those decisions may well have been over-reactions.

REFERENCES

1. Lynn, M. (1994) Redundancies focus on the white-collar worker. *Sunday Times*, 20th March.
2. Kay, H. (1994) Workers pay a heavy price for recovery. *Independent on Sunday*, 27th February.
3. KPMG (1992) Survey of Career Counselling/Outplacement and Career Management. London: KPMG.
4. Coulson-Thomas, C. and Coe, T. (1991) *The Flat Organisation: Philosophy and Practice*. Corby: BIM Press.
5. Wheatley, M. (1992) *The Future of Middle Management*. Corby: BIM Press.
6. MSL International (1994) MSL Index.
7. Wakelam, A. and Teberler, M. (1993) *The Effects of the Recession on Management Structure and Organisation*. Centre for Management Studies, University of Exeter.
8. Inkson, K. and Coe, T. (1993) *Are Career Ladders Disappearing?* Corby: Institute of Management.
9. Nicholson, N. and West, M. (1988) *Managerial Job Change: Men and Women in Transition*. Cambridge: Cambridge University Press.
10. Coe, T. (1993) *Managers Under Stress*. Corby: Institute of Management.
11. Priority Management Systems, Inc. (1993) *The Values Gap*, 1993.

12. Herriot, P., Pemberton, C. and Hawtin, E. (1995) The career attitudes and intentions of managers in the finance sector. *British Journal of Management* (in press).

Chapter Two

THE NEW VOCABULARY

While journalists may have painted an over-simplified picture, they are certainly telling some of it like it is. The same cannot be said for those in power in organizations. They are telling most of it like it isn't.

A whole new language has developed over the last fifteen years, a form of management-speak which actively seeks to misrepresent the reality[1]. Seeking to sanitize the unpleasant facts, organizations are awash with Orwellian double-speak. Here are a few of the new words, together with the definitions intended by their users and the cynical definitions preferred by some of their recipients:

♦ *Downsizing*
  - eliminating over-manning, thereby increasing productivity
  - sacking people
♦ *Rightsizing*
  - eliminating over-manning with great precision, thereby
  - sacking people

> maximally increasing
> productivity

- ♦ *Lean and Mean*
  - fighting fit to win the   – mean
    competitive battle
- ♦ *Flexibility*
  - rapidly adapting human   – taking away my expertise;
    resource supply to changing   or putting people on
    business demands   part-time
- ♦ *Empowerment*
  - passing authority to take   – more responsibility, same
    decisions down the line to   rewards
    those who deal with customers
- ♦ *Commitment*
  - sharing the organization's – brain-washing
    values and buying in to its
    vision and mission
- ♦ *Culture Change*
  - persuading people to share – brain-washing
    the organization's values, etc.
- ♦ *Vision and Mission*
  - what the organization might – delusional fantasies
    become in the future, and
    what its core purpose is
- ♦ *Human Resources*
  - our people, working   – a new-fangled American
    together to achieve   name for personnel
    business objectives
- ♦ *Self-development*
  - the responsibility of all to   – removal of what little
    learn and develop themselves training we get

HUMAN RESOURCE MANAGEMENT: THE PROJECT

Underlying these light-hearted "definitions" lurks a more serious question. Do these items of "management-speak" form part of a new language? If so, does this new language describe a coherent new set of policies and practices? Or is the reality a lot more confused and messy than the language implies?

In its starkest form, the Human Resource Management language looks at people as another form of economic asset[2]. Employees are seen as a human capital resource and, like all organizational resources, are there to enable the organization to achieve its business objectives. All of the structural changes—downsizing, delayering, outsourcing, etc.— and all of the new systems and processes—performance-related pay, culture change programmes, etc.—have a single purpose. They are designed to enable the organization to achieve its business objectives. To this end, all of the systems are consistent with each other; and they all contribute to a Human Resource Strategy which is itself an inherent part of the Business Strategy[3]. So runs the rhetoric.

The use of the language of assets and resources is very significant. It implies ownership and use. People belong to and are used by the organization. They may be developed and grown, but equally they may be discarded as the situation demands[4]. Of course, the language of Human Resource Management is prescriptive rather than descriptive. It is based upon a largely American project which aims to establish the organization's business success as the only worthwhile goal. It assumes that such success will be achieved by controlling people at work; that the interests and values of individuals and the organization should be identical; and that their commitment to the organization will therefore be assured. From commitment will follow increased effort and improved performance. Indeed, employees will be willing to go the extra mile, since they will be driven by their internalized values rather than by their employment contract[5]. Transformational charismatic leaders and committed line managers will ensure that Human Resource Management is effectively practised. And finally, it is practised on individuals—collective representation is out of the window.

HUMAN RESOURCE MANAGEMENT: THE FACTS

So runs the rhetoric of tough HRM (there is a tender version, too!). Does it describe what's really happening? Are downsizing and delayering part of an integrated plan aimed at achieving business goals? Emphatically not. Just as the downsizing of managers and professionals is patchy, so these other career-related policies and practices are introduced piecemeal and reactively. They are often jettisoned like last year's fashion because they haven't "done the trick". Human Resource Management serves as a post-hoc rationalization for these events. Rather than swallow its alarming rhetoric, we need to look at the evidence.

That evidence is in remarkable agreement. Those who have conducted serious research in this area in the UK have come up with similar findings. Take, for example, the detailed investigation of 15 mainstream organizations by John Storey and colleagues[6]. By "mainstream", these researchers meant large organizations which were not often-quoted flagships for Human Resource Management (such as Rank Xerox, Hewlett-Packard or Nissan). Rather, they represented a pragmatic approach with, often, a history of collective agreements with trade unions. They were investigated by interviews at different levels and on different sites, and were rated along 25 key dimensions of Human Resource Management. These included:

♦ Beliefs and assumptions
    e.g. – all have the same interests
         – values and/or mission are explicit
♦ Strategic aspects
    e.g. – customer orientation
         – speedy decision-making
♦ Line managers
    e.g. – facilitation is valued
         – transformational leadership
♦ Key levers
    e.g. – teamworking
         – performance-related pay
         – increased communication

Some of the 25 features were present in all or nearly all of the 15 organizations; for example

♦ Business need as the prime guide to action
♦ Values/mission

♦ Customer orientation
♦ Line managers to the fore

However, these features co-existed with the older tradition of representation: relatively few organizations assumed identity of interest between organization and employees or a move to individual contracts (across the workforce). Furthermore, there was little evidence of the much-vaunted integration of policies. Rather, it may well be the case that the Human Resource Management phenomenon "is in reality a symbolic label behind which lurk multifarious practices, many of which are not mutually dependent upon each other"[7]. This is hardly surprising—some practices, for example individual performance-related pay and teamwork, are mutually contradictory! Moreover, while some organizations (e.g. Rover, Whitbread) had embraced nearly all the features, others (e.g. Smith & Nephew) had taken few on board. Yet the degree of conformity bore minimal relationship to financial success, or to employee commitment, trust and satisfaction.

Other research supports these findings. There was little innovative reorganization of work during the 1980s; communication was still top-down; there was a big gap between espoused and actual policy; and there were still strong financial and other constraints on managers' decision-making[8].

Has the end of the recession changed this picture? Is there a brave new HR world emerging from the pain? The most recent research[9] indicates that the picture is still a confused one. Shaun Tyson and Michael Witcher surveyed a sample of 30 from the FTSE top 1000 companies. They were all large British companies, from engineering, retail, leisure, pharmaceuticals, utilities and conglomerate sectors. They included BAT, BOC, BT, Cadbury Schweppes, ICI, Laporte, Marks and Spencer, National Grid, Racal, Forte, and Wellcome.

The authors found:

1. Some organizations engaged in the formulation of long-term HR strategy, often allocating this task to a central planning unit.
2. More coupled HR and business much more loosely, changing them at divisional level to accord with customer or competitor changes.

3. Others still simply reacted to events with individual and unrelated responses, then rationalized them post-hoc and dignified them with strategic content.

Overall, these researchers conclude that the scene is one of flexibility and localization of response and the relative absence of long-term plans. Instead, efforts to engineer the engagement of "hearts, minds and particular behaviours" continue apace.

In sum, organizations have adopted a pick and mix approach. What is certainly the case is that they have imposed a great deal of change on all employees, and especially on managers. Thus, while managers traditionally saw themselves as managing change rather than as its victims, they are now in the firing line themselves. Finding themselves suddenly at the receiving end, most of them do not have the protection of unions. Watch out for the coming proletarianized professionals! The gamekeepers have become poachers, but the game is scarce. In the next chapter, we explore the realities from their point of view. We will argue that the real revolution is not the move from fusty old Personnel to shiny new Human Resources; it is in the psychological contract between managers and professionals and their organizations.

REFERENCES

1. Cohen, N. and Trapp, R. (1994) The New English Babble. *Independent on Sunday*, 12th June.
2. Hendry, C. and Pettigrew, A. (1990) Human resource management: An agenda for the 1990s. *International Journal of Human Resource Management*, **1**, 1, 17–44.
3. Fombrun, C. J., Tichy, N. M. and Devanna, M. A. (1985) *Strategic Human Resource Management*. New York: John Wiley.
4. Keenoy, T. (1990) HRM: A case of the wolf in sheep's clothing? *Personnel Review*, **19**, 2, 3–9.
5. Willmott, H. (1993) Strength is ignorance; slavery is freedom. Managing culture in modern organizations. *Journal of Management Studies*, **30**, 4, 515–552.
6. Storey, J. (1992) HRM in action: The truth is out at last. *Personnel Management*, **24**, 4, 28–31.

7. Ibid., p.31.
8. Marginson, P., Edwards, P. K., Martin, R., Purcell, J. and Sisson, K. (1988) *Beyond the Workplace*. Oxford: Basil Blackwell.
9. Tyson, S. and Witcher, M. (1994) Getting in gear: post-recession HR management. *Personnel Management*, **26**, 8, 20–23.

Chapter Three

DEALS OLD AND NEW

THE OLD DEAL

You might have supposed from our account so far that employment consists of a series of experiences which organizations put
"their" people through. Those people may be construed as assets, if
they are lucky, or as costs if they are not. But in either case, they are
seen by the organization as its property.

As far as the individual is concerned (and, to be fair, many organizations, too), nobody owns them. Despite the Human Resource
Management project, the employment relationship is contractual, as
it always has been since slavery was outlawed[1]. No one owes their
soul to the company store or to the company (though it may feel like
it to those with subsidized mortgages).

A contract is between two parties, who each give undertakings to
the other. The legal contract of employment makes these undertakings explicit, and formalizes the agreement of the two parties to its
terms. Yet there is another contract, the psychological contract,
which exists in the minds of the parties[2]. This may never have been

made explicit in words or writing, but this does not mean that it does not exist. Perceptions are real. Twenty years ago, anyone who worked in a bank or insurance company *knew* that the psychological contract was loyalty in exchange for security. It was never spelled out, but there was no need to spell it out. Everyone could see the way the bank looked after the deputy manager who had shot his bolt but still had five years to go.

Of course, this implicit nature of many psychological contracts left the parties vulnerable to misunderstandings[3]. In particular, it's hard to read the mind of "the organization". Several different organizational members may represent it where the individual's career is concerned—their line manager, the personnel director and the chief executive, for example. Annual appraisals managed by the line manager may be sending different messages from career plans formulated by the personnel director[4].

Nevertheless, most people seem to have a fairly clear idea what the deal is: what the organization offers to meet their needs and what they offer to meet the organization's needs. To demonstrate that we all have some notion of the psychological contract, draw up two columns, representing what you offered your organization and what your organization offered you. We have used the past tense because we are asking you first to complete these columns as they were ten years ago. In 1985, or even more in 1975, if you can remember that far back, what was the nature of the deal?

Perhaps you came up with something like this:

You offered
- Loyalty—not leaving
- Conformity—doing what you were asked
- Commitment—going the extra mile
- Trust—they'll keep their promises

Organization offered
- Security of employment
- Promotion prospects

- Training and development

- Care in trouble

THE EXTRA MILE

The word "relationship" seems to describe this deal rather better than the word "contract". Each of the parties trusted the other to complete their side of an exchange, even when they had themselves already fulfilled their own side of the bargain. Organizations, for example, would invest considerable sums in a general management trainee programme for graduates, confident that most of them would stay and repay the investment. Graduates would spend several years in trainee grade, confident that promotion would come their way in time[5].

But it's going the extra mile, on both sides, that really captures the nature of the old deal. Here's two examples[6], one at the early and one at the final stages of the relationship.

> Quite recently, there was a young man who won our regional "employee of the year" award. It is well worth having. Our regional winner wouldn't have anything to do with it, and repeatedly refused his invitation to the **** hotel. Eventually, somebody found out that he was stony broke, and was too embarrassed to attend the national ceremony in scruffy old clothes. When the man's manager heard about this he bought the fellow a very smart suit of clothes out of his own pocket. Our man did not win the national title but he received a magnificent cut-glass rose bowl as his award. He was less excited by the bowl than he was with his clothes. He wanted to give the bowl to the manager, but of course he would not accept it.
>
> A very unusual act of loyalty comes to mind of a man who accepted a career promotion elsewhere, only for his colleague, who was the second half of a very important duo, to die very suddenly. This man then went to his new employer, explained the circumstances and negotiated a three-month delay to his starting date. This gave us vital breathing space and we were able to release him after two months. We paid him his enhanced salary, and offered his new employer a recognition payment. They were gracious enough to decline, but their agreement to the deferment was of immense help to us. The credit must go to the loyalty of our erstwhile employee who did not want to see us damaged.

So the old deal was often a real relationship, which cemented over time. The parties learned to trust each other more as they each found that the other fulfilled their side of the bargain. Mutual loyalty and commitment meant that if either was in trouble, the other would help out, regardless of whether this help would be rewarded or reciprocated. Of course, there were downsides too: as with so many relationships, the parties could start taking each other for granted[6].

> Our branch network changed to a live, on-line computer system. One member of each branch was nominated to receive training, then training in training, so that he could go back and train all the staff at his home branch. It was a very heavy commitment placed on the trainers. They often had to commute long and difficult journeys, attend residential courses and provide feedback on the branch staff's progress. The day came and the change occurred in one fell swoop. Other than a few minor hitches, it all went well. After all this effort there was just a perfunctory two-sentence notice from Head Office to say that the system had gone live, and to thank staff for their endeavours. This was fair enough for branch staff and the likes of me, but it was not good enough for the trainers. They should have had special recognition, a special pay supplement and personal letters. What would it have taken to mail-merge a standard letter with personalized addresses on a word processor? These trainers had to be, by the very nature of the task, some of our brightest young people. Many of them have since left, and part of the reason is because the firm just doesn't care.

THE NEW DEAL

And employees can take their firm for granted, too; they may expect security and salary rises regardless of effort and performance. Overall, though, the old deal seemed satisfactory to both parties—a fair exchange. The ties that bind were not a straitjacket for many—more a happy and comfortable marriage: growing old together.

For all sorts of reasons which we will discuss later, the old deal has gone for ever. What has taken its place? We suggest you do the same exercise as before, but this time describe your present experience. What is your *current* deal with your employer?

Perhaps your response looks something like this:

You offer
♦ Long hours

Organization offers
♦ High pay

- Added responsibility
- Broader skills
- Tolerance of change and ambiguity

- Rewards for performance
- A job

Comparisons are painful. We'll look at feelings in the next chapter, but there is one crucial distinction we want to make here[7]. The new deal isn't *relational* any more. There's no taking on trust, no mutual commitment. The new deal is a strictly *transactional* one; you give me this and I'll give you that. Indeed, without too much effort an accountant could make a useful stab at turning the whole thing into a balance sheet: productivity and pay as pounds and pence. Some of them have tried already.

It's worth reflecting on the nature of transactional deals. What is it that makes them so different from relational ones?

- Parties don't go beyond the contract
- Parties check that the terms are being fulfilled
- Changes in the contract are explicitly negotiated or imposed
- Commitment is calculative[8]

So there are no extra miles being gone here, no loyalty and affection. I calculate whether I'd gain or lose if I left, rather than sticking by the organization through thick and thin. And just as they spend their time checking up on my productivity, so I'll check up on them; my performance-related pay had better tally to the nth decimal point.

REFERENCES

1. Willmott, H. (1993) Strength is ignorance; slavery is freedom. Managing culture in modern organizations. *Journal of Management Studies*, **30**, 4, 515–552.
2. Rousseau, D. M. and Parks, J. M. (1993) The contracts of individuals and organizations. In Cummings, L. L. and Staw, B. M. (eds) *Research in Organizational Behavior*, Vol. 15. Greenwich CT: JAI Press.
3. Herriot, P., Pemberton, C. and Pinder, R. (1994) Misperceptions by managers and their bosses of each other's preferences regarding the

managers' careers: A case of the blind leading the blind? *Human Resource Management Journal*, **4**, 2, 39–51.

4. Hirsh, W. (1990) *Succession Planning: Current Practice and Future Issues.* Brighton: Institute of Manpower Studies.

5. Herriot, P. (1984) *Down from the Ivory Tower: Graduates and their Jobs.* Chichester: John Wiley.

6. Manning, W. E. G. (1993) The content of the psychological contract between employees and organizations in Great Britain in the early 1990s. PhD thesis, University of London.

7. Rousseau, D. M. (1990) New hire perceptions of their own and their employer's obligations: A study of psychological contracts. *Journal of Organizational Behavior*, **11**, 5, 389–400.

8. Meyer, J. P. and Allen, N. J. (1984) Testing the "side-bet" theory of organizational commitment: some methodological considerations. *Journal of Applied Psychology*, **69**, 372–378.

Chapter Four

IT'S NOT FAIR

THE LOSS OF THE OLD

Any sort of contract involves *exchange*; the psychological contracts of 1985 and 1995 in the previous chapter had two columns—what individuals offer, and what organizations offer. Contracts also imply a *promise*—to fulfil one's own side of the bargain (provided, of course, that the other party fulfils theirs)[1]. Exchanges and promises carry a lot of emotional baggage. We are very concerned that the exchange is a fair one, and feel highly aggrieved when it isn't. As for promises, God help the one who breaks them; they are not to be trusted (ever again)![2]

People buying houses are prime examples. They haggle endlessly over relatively small sums on the basis of what the house is worth (compared to similar ones). And hell hath no fury like a buyer gazumped (or a seller left in the lurch).

Exactly the same is true of the psychological contract. Is the deal a fair one? asks the employee. How was it negotiated, or was it just imposed? Has the organization kept its side of the bargain? These are issues of great concern to any employee at any time. In the middle of the contractual revolution, they are paramount.

Many managers have experienced the whole gamut. They have, for a start, seen the old psychological contract unilaterally broken. Even organizations which had explicitly offered jobs for life (IBM) reluctantly reneged on the contract. For many more, the implicit contract of security and promotion was shattered by the downsizing and delayering of the 80s and 90s. The consequence was anger and loss of trust. As a manager in a financial institution put it to us:

> I have to comment that ***** has destroyed motivation, loyalty and trust, and has a long way to go to restore staff relationships— if it cares! I feel so pressured, threatened and insecure that despite your assurances to the contrary I am not a hundred per cent convinced that my identity will not reach *****. I don't think it will be too difficult to establish who I am from the personal statistics completed on your form.

(Respondents had been assured that their questionnaires would not be sent to their organization.)

Feelings of inequity followed on from the redundancies, and not just among those made redundant. Reflecting on the injustice of colleagues being jettisoned after a lifetime's service, an insurance company manager muses:

> The company should be fairer with senior management. It has changed interpretation of contracts, particularly in relation to redundancy. Management are now treated less favourably than staff, and many who have served the company well are being judged against much tougher standards. Many of these managers are at an age where new jobs are difficult to find in the current recession, yet because of previous company policy have mortgages which run to age 60. The company should have a more humane approach and is building up a lot of bitterness amongst its management group. A number close to retirement cannot wait to get out. Staff made redundant should be given more thought, especially in relation to the actual procedure.

This manager isn't just concerned about *what* has been done—he's angry about *how* it was done[3]. This is just what you expect when a relationship is broken—we need it to be done in a kindly way so that we are at least assured that the relationship meant something to the other person.

> Some of the people are ushered out of here coldly, like it's all over and you can't even say goodbye to your friends. They come here and clean off their desks at night. All of a sudden the desk is clear; it's gone. They've disappeared. They've vanished into the woodwork[4].

And apart from the manner of their going, there's the decision itself and its communication. How were people selected for redundancy and on what basis? Were the criteria communicated? How was the decision broken to them? How much notice were they given? Did they receive outplacement help? What sort of a financial deal did they get?

And there's the rub. When it's possible to make comparisons, feelings of injustice boil over. How can it possibly be fair for a lifetime's service to be rewarded with a moderate redundancy package and short shrift when those who are responsible to shareholders for the (mis)management of the company are given obscenely large golden parachutes? Consider the following recent pay-offs:

Name	Company	Payoff
Ernest Mario	Glaxo	£4 000 000
John Cahill	British Aerospace	£3 200 000
Jim Maxim	Laura Ashley	£1 200 000
Tom Garvin	United Biscuits	£932 000
Crispin Davis	Guinness	£670 000
Richard Young	Midlands Electricity	£655 000
Jonathan Agnew	Kleinwort Benson	£600 000
John Bellak	Severn Trent Water	£513 000
Cedric Scroggs	Fisons	£417 000

Inadequate compensation for a career's service is one thing; seeing those whom you blame for your plight, rightly or wrongly, being given a fortune is quite another. Comparisons are odious, and these, they feel, stink to high heaven.

THE IMPOSITION OF THE NEW

But what of the new contract? How do managers feel about its process and its content? The first gripe is that it wasn't entered into willingly, but was *imposed*. Managers are very clear that they were forced into the new deal by their lack of labour-market power in a period of recession[5]. The generous offer of a job by the organization is part of the new deal. Here's how two managers from the same financial organization feel about it:

> ***** is like any large organization which exudes strength and stability in times of recession. The organization can make great demands on its staff and reduce career opportunities for its workforce whilst giving those who remain more responsibility and a greater volume of work. It is safe in the knowledge that staff will respond, due to fear of unemployment and lack of prospects elsewhere. Only when the economic climate becomes less oppressive will the pendulum swing from *****'s attitude of "Do it or else" to one of worrying about staff turnover and nurturing loyalty instead of abusing it! Sorry to appear cynical but I have never responded to being bullied!

> Management are more and more being put in a "no win" situation, i.e. measured on performance when they have no control over targets or resources. Due to the recession, companies know that management are unlikely to resign or complain; therefore they just pile on the pressure. This is not a good practice as they lose management to illness, or demotivate them so much that they work to a minimum standard.

These quotations spell out the consequences for the organization of making managers feel powerless. Anger at having a contract imposed is compounded with a feeling of powerlessness to be able to do anything about it. All that's left for them is to accept the retreat from the relational to the transactional contract and act accordingly. "Right," they say to themselves, "if that's the new deal, then I'm sticking to the letter of the new law. No more going the extra mile from now on."

But they say it only to themselves. They carry on with their act because they are afraid. They can't "work to rule" in a formal way since they have no history of representation. If the present contract continues, we will see the further growth of such unions as the Banking Insurance and Finance Union (BIFU) and the Manufacturing Science and Finance Union (MSF). The managers and the professionals will become the new proletariat!

What of the new deal itself; how fair is it? As with all contracts that are imposed by one party, the deal appears to favour that party. It is basically an inequitable exchange in the eyes of the other, particularly compared with the good old times.

Here's a blunt statement from an insurance manager: the same from them, and more from me!

> The pace of change over the last eighteen months has been so great that my job is unrecognizable now to the one I was doing before. It is too early to know how I will benefit—my salary is no bigger now than it was eighteen months ago despite *much* more responsibility; it's just that the job title has changed. I need to see evidence that anything has really changed.

What's more, there are hidden costs to individuals which aren't part of the new contract, but which it necessarily involves:

> Consistently being expected to work in excess of 47 hours per week, often much more, excluding short or non-existent lunch breaks, is "burning out" many senior staff. Many are taking extra early retirement or relinquishing their jobs because of the impact it is having on their private lives and their health. In my case, 30+ years' loyalty is being pushed beyond breaking point. Ominously, younger staff on the first or second rung of management are relinquishing because of the pressure, which does not augur well for the future. The high level of stress-related illness, extra early retirements, relinquishments, etc. must be indicating something to the Executive!

Again, these have knock-on effects for the organization; for the first time we are seeing the emergence of "the reluctant managers"[6]. Many of today's managers do not aspire to the few promotions that remain:

> Career aspirations are virtually nil. I've seen my line manager's job description, his workload, his desk—and he can keep it. Similarly, my subordinates are taking a jaundiced view of career

progression and weighing up the rewards/cost ratio in terms of how much is extra money worth in relation to longer hours (mostly unpaid) and greater stress levels. This, of course, is a great pity. People should want to come to work and perform for the organization and have adequate resources to do so instead of constantly having to juggle increasing workloads with fewer staff. On a temporary basis that is fine, but it is now becoming an everyday part of the culture. There is no scope for personal input; everything is centrally planned. I personally am prepared to stand (or fall) by what I can deliver, provided I have some input to targeting, admin levels, budget and resource management. Until that unlikely day arrives, the only planning I am doing is for my retirement. I believe I have a lot to offer but "they" know best. As I said, a great pity.

Finally, we come to the pathetic instance of someone who feels they have to go on a part-time contract in order to do a full-time job (rather than a double-time one):

> Promotion was a slight possibility before but has disappeared whilst I work part-time, I believe. In fact, because of family commitments, I would prefer less responsibility, not more; therefore part-time work on one grade lower is acceptable. My salary (pro rata) is protected and I do not believe I will really do any different tasks, but "officially" I will be less responsible. In practice, the organization knows they will receive the same commitment but on fewer days of the week. The main reason for wanting part-time work is that full-time is much more than a basic week—up to fifty hours and call-out situations at night/weekends and also short-notice extra working. Offering me a part-time contract is the only way my employers believe they can allow me to avoid these extra burdens whilst expecting other employees to continue in the same vein.

So, many managers are very angry. They feel they have been unjustly treated:

♦ In the breaking of the old contract
♦ In the way it was broken
♦ In the unfair compensation paid

♦ In the unilateral imposition of the new contract
♦ In the unfair deal it contains

Now imagine how they feel when, under the banner of Human Resource Management, they are urged to commit themselves body, soul and spirit to their organization and its new values. Only those, they feel, with the sensitivity and imagination of a warthog would fail to perceive that this could be a counter-productive project!

Commitment is mutual. It partly derives from mutual trust built up over time[7]. Trust depends upon promises being honoured. It cannot be induced by one-off culture-change programmes. Trust is earned; it cannot be induced. To quote a manager from a recently privatized utility: "Things have reached a stage where no one trusts the words any more and the actions have proved false."

So there's a perspective from the managerial trenches. Many have made a hot response, understandably reacting in terms of their strong feelings of inequity and injustice. Their perspective is that of their own career experiences and aspirations. What is the point of view from HQ? What are the reasons for the revolution in the psychological contract? How have organizations differed in their responses to these pressures?

REFERENCES

1. Rousseau, D. M. and Parks, J. M. (1993) The contracts of individuals and organizations. In Cummings, L. L. and Staw, B. M. (eds) *Research in Organizational Behavior*, Vol. 15. Greenwich, CT: JAI Press.
2. Herriot, P., Gibbons, P., Pemberton, C. and Jackson, P. R. (1994) An empirical model of managerial careers in organizations. *British Journal of Management*, 5, 113–121.
3. McFarlin, D. B. and Sweeney, P. D. (1992) Distributive and procedural justice as predictors of satisfaction with personal and organizational outcomes. *Academy of Management Journal*, 35, 3, 626–637.
4. Noer, D. M. (1993) *Healing the Wounds*. San Francisco: Jossey-Bass.
5. Barney, J. B. and Lawrence, B. S. (1989) Pinstripes, power ties and personal relationships: The economics of career strategy. In Arthur, M. B., Hall, D. T. and Lawrence, B. S. (eds) *Handbook of Career Theory*. Cambridge: Cambridge University Press.

6. Scase, R. and Goffee, R. (1989) *Reluctant Managers: Their Work and Lifestyles*. London: Unwin Hyman.
7. Moorman, R. M. (1991) The relationship between organizational justice and organizational citizenship behaviours: Do fairness perceptions influence employee citizenship? *Journal of Applied Psychology*, **76**, 845–855.

Part Two

WHY IS IT HAPPENING?

Chapter Five

GLOBAL TRENDS

ABB: A EUROPEAN MULTINATIONAL

In August 1994, Sir Iain Vallance announced yet another programme of job cuts in British Telecommunications plc[1]. The previous round of redundancies had not yet been completed, yet here, in a year of record profits, further reductions in the managerial ranks were announced. Despite Vallance's repeated and praiseworthy attempts to explain his reasons, those now threatened are often unable to understand why they are yet again at risk. Indeed, at a meeting bravely called by management: "The graduate employees, the rank and file and the middle managers spoke with one voice: they felt betrayed, put-upon, unloved and angry"[2].

Why is it all happening? What are the reasons for this revolution in managers' and professionals' employment relations? What's the perspective of those who are responsible to shareholders for the running of the business? Are they a bunch of mean sadists who get their kicks out of sacking people or squeezing them dry? Despite their foolish use of such weasel words as "lean and mean" or "right-sizing", the top people in organizations are not, in general, sadistic or cruel. Rather, they see themselves being forced to boost efficiency and productivity in the interests of corporate and personal survival. So hostile has the competition become that any new system or solution which promises to increase cost-competitiveness has been seized upon avidly by top management.

It's instructive to look at the current organizational darling of the business press—Asea Brown Boveri (ABB). Its Chief Executive, Percy Barnevik, had previously headed Asea, the Swedish electrical engineering and robotics giant. As soon as he was appointed there, he reduced the central staff from 1700 to 200 in about 100 days. Asea merged with the Swiss Brown Boveri in 1987, and he reduced the Brown Boveri HQ from 4000 to 200. What happened to them? One third were redundant, one third went to units of the company in the marketplace, and one third were asked to sell their services profitably inside or outside the organization. Now there are only 150 people in ABB's corporate HQ—100 professionals and 50 administrative staff. These latter are separated from Barnevik, their CEO, by only three hierarchical layers.

Not only has he stripped down corporate staffing; he has also divided the business up into at least 5000 different units, each of them a profit centre. On average, each unit employs only 40 people. This process, too, involved downsizing—1000 per month in 1993[3]. Barnevik's reasons for this devolution of responsibility are explicit. He believes that only small units have the flexibility and energy to meet customers' needs faster and more effectively than their competitors. Since he thinks that markets are more and more crowded with competitors, such sources of competitive advantage are to be treasured and cherished.

ABB is the largest power engineering group in the world. Its 1993 annual turnover of $28.3 billion was derived from Western Europe, Asia and the Americas. It operates in 140 countries, and develops products in at least 12. Recently, ABB, together with Marks and Spencer, were rated by top executives as the most respected European company regardless of sector. The main reason for this award was their strategic excellence, identified as push into growth markets, reducing fixed costs and reducing net debt (with consequent shareholder benefit). Especially instructive were the reasons for the

Asea and Brown Boveri merger: increasing privatization and de-regulation meant that each of the two organizations would be unlikely to survive the subsequent shakeout on its own.

Senior executives in UK companies have faced all the threats which ABB has apparently surmounted. Unlike Sweden and Switzerland, however, UK companies have little recent national history of overseas marketing and collaboration. Moreover, as we will argue in the next chapter, they face in addition a set of constraints which make it even harder for them to compete.

ASIAN COMPETITION

The impact of the success of the Pacific rim countries in comparison with Europe and North America has been huge[4]. With their low labour costs and high productivity, many of their organizations have become global. They sell on price and quality/reliability—value for money.

Some Western organizations, but only a few, have succeeded in competing on these terms. By producing in low-wage economies, reducing distribution costs to a minimum, acquiring global brands and marketing locally with effective local sales forces, organizations such as Grand Metropolitan have enhanced their market share in branded consumables.

These organizations have achieved economies of scale by their multiplant, multinational activities, and economies in the scope of their operations because their products are related to each other. Many UK organizations have sought to emulate the drive to reduce costs and increase productivity, while being unable or unwilling to become multinational. In concentrating on the need to be cost-competitive, these latter organizations have (perhaps unknowingly) agreed with Michael Porter's rather static dictum: you can compete on cost-competitiveness, or you can compete by innovating into niche markets, but you can't do both at the same time[5].

As a huge generalization, very many larger UK companies find themselves with cash cows: products or services which give them a big share of slow or static (and mainly domestic) markets. Their natural response has been to seek to compete by cost leadership, by:

♦ Exercising tight controls on expenditure
♦ Close supervision
♦ Setting quantitative targets
♦ Individual performance-related pay[6]

In other words, many UK companies have sought to become cost-competitive without the advantages of the economies which multinational activity brings.

However, they have also realized that the competition, especially that from the Far East, has more to offer than simply cheaper goods. Multinational firms are seen to "think globally but act locally". They are seen to differentiate their products or services to suit local markets or individual tastes. What's more, many of them are astonishingly quick to make these adaptations. They have reduced time to market amazingly. Positively Stakhanovite efforts are made in the Tiger economies. Consider the case of microwave ovens[7].

At a time when Japanese and American manufacturers were selling 4 million microwave ovens a year, Yun Soo Chu, an engineer of the Samsung Corporation of Korea, started trying to make one for himself. He spent many months, and had two major disasters, working 80 hours per week. Eventually he succeeded, and J. C. Penney, a US retail chain, put in an order, hoping to sell the Korean product for less than $300.

In order to meet deadlines for the order, Samsung executives and engineers had to design and build assembly lines from scratch. They worked 20 hours a day for weeks on end to do so. In one year, production increased from 1000 to over 100 000 ovens.

Soon, Japanese and American competitors brought their prices down as a result of technological sophistication. The Koreans responded by making the most technologically advanced component, the magnet, themselves. Hitherto, they had outsourced it to Japan. They now began to compete with Matsushita of Japan for supplying smaller ovens to General Electric (who were outsourcing production). GE invited a proposal, including a cost breakdown, delivery schedule and production plan. Instead of the normal 4–6 weeks wait, GE received the proposal the next morning. It was presented by a group of exhausted engineers: they had worked all night.

Typically, operatives at Samsung work 11 hours a day, 27 days a month. Engineers work 68 hours a week. When asked why, they say they want to improve their lifestyle; by "lifestyle", they mean what they own. And they want it for their children, too.

It is when they are faced with such attitudes and behaviour as this that Western executives get the jitters. A few continue to believe that this level of cost competition only applies to some sectors of manufacturing. More, however, are appalled by the general implications. Customers now expect ever cheaper products or services, of ever-higher quality. They are being provided with them by foreign companies with low-cost labour, high productivity, a fanatical concern for the customer and for quality, and amazing speed to market. Senior executives fear for their cash cows, be they products or services. They cut costs to the bone, put their heads down and hope that Porter was right.

IS COST-COMPETITIVENESS ENOUGH?

Yet when they look at the ABBs of this world, the doubts start creeping in. For ABB not only cut its costs; it colonized new markets as well. It won its prize in the *Financial Times* Survey of most respected companies for pushing into growth markets, as well as for reducing fixed costs and nett debt[3]. Many UK companies recognize that cost-competitiveness is not enough. High value-added, up-market, well-differentiated products and services which either meet or create customer needs are also required in the long run. Yet so powerful are the added pressures facing UK businesses that this prospect remains a pipe dream for most.

It's when they read the Harvard professors' analysis of true transnational success[8], however, that their spirits really drop. Add the efficiency of electronics to the niche marketing of branded goods and you've still not got enough. You need the transfer of knowledge across the worldwide organization for real innovation[9]. Faced with the intimidating examples of successful competitors and the earnest exhortations of the gurus, who can blame executives for feeling threatened? They are between the devil and the deep blue sea: face the rigours of global competition for global markets, or fight for a share of a static domestic market.

BOOM AND BUST

Yet the savage competition unleashed by deregulation and privatization is only one of their problems. Another is the increase in the frequency, size and unpredictability of the economic cycle. Bigger booms follow bigger busts ever faster. The 1980–82 recession was followed by a period of stability, with 1986–88 moving into the Lawson boom. Then, suddenly, down into recession in 1989–91, with a double whammy into 1992 and 93. In August 1994, the CBI, the Institute of Directors and the Bank of England all regarded the recovery as fragile, depending upon a delicate balance between interest rates and inflation. In such a context, the longer-term investment and planning required to enter new markets with new products and services is unattractive to larger organizations. They leave it to the small new businesses which their more innovative staff leave to set up. They cannot afford to carry any "surplus" staff not devoted to providing the product or service and adding value to the bottom line. Rather, they push resources into marketing and selling, often disregarding service quality; witness recent judgements against financial service organizations by the regulatory body IMRO.

IT AND CONTROL

Finally, there are some long-term structural changes to which senior executives are having to adapt, some of them leading inexorably, it seems, to a strategy of cost-competitiveness. Consider, for example, the onward march of information technology (IT). The major purpose to which IT has been successfully put is undoubtedly that of control: control of the manufacturing process; or of expenditure; or of the entire business cycle (in the case of retail food stores)[10]. Sometimes, the control is exercised within isolated processes or functions; occasionally it's integrated across all business activities;

very rarely, business processes are radically redesigned to exploit IT capabilities[11].

In all these cases, the claim is made that IT reduces costs. While the evidence of short-term cost savings is ambivalent, the attraction of IT as a means of control is only too clear. Its potential for innovation remains largely untapped. When technology promises cost reduction, the reasons for choosing cost-competitiveness as the strategic aim are enhanced.

PART-TIMERS

There are other structural developments in Western labour markets, too, which make cost-competitiveness an attractive strategy. The proportion of all adult women participating in the UK labour market has increased from 47 per cent in 1963 through 53 per cent in 1973, 58 per cent in 1983, to 68 per cent in 1990. In 1990, 44 per cent of women's jobs were part-time, compared with only 5 per cent of men's jobs[12]. The opportunity to use part-time, poorly paid female labour to meet peak demand has been enhanced by the number of early retirees who want or need to continue earning. By 1992, 24 per cent of the entire UK workforce were in part-time employment. Between March and September 1993, a staggering 113 000 full-time jobs vanished and 210 000 part-time jobs were created. Projections of current trends indicate that within ten years, half of all jobs will be part-time. This increased availability of part-time labour, common to most countries in Europe, is yet another reason for Western firms to aim for cost-competitiveness as a main strategic response.

So to return to Sir Ian Vallance of BT, with whom we started this chapter. He would argue that BT is entering into global competition for an immense global market. Its competitors are mostly young organizations without BT's history. That history is one of a heavily unionized nationalized industry adapted to a national market only. Now it faces international competitors such as AT & T which became deregulated earlier in time, and therefore have had a head start in the competitive race. Seen from the perspective of the global electronic highway, the individuals who lose their jobs, and those who remain to do the work of two, are unfortunate but necessary casualties in the competitive war. Seen from the trenches rather than the command post, the view is rather different.

REFERENCES

1. Adonis, A. (1994) BT plans to shed 50 000 more jobs. *Financial Times*, August 1st.
2. Kellaway, L. (1994) Betrayed, unloved and angry. *Financial Times*, August 1st.
3. Taylor, P. and Martin, P. (1994) Customer loyalty and clear policy top agenda. *Financial Times*, June 27th.
4. IPM (1993) Managing People—The Changing Frontiers. Institute of Personnel Management Consultative Document. London: IPM Press.
5. Porter, M. (1985) *Competitive Advantage*. New York: Free Press.
6. McKinlay, A. and Starkey, K. (1992) Strategy and human resource management. *International Journal of Human Resource Management*, **3**, 3, 435–450.
7. Magaziner, I. C. and Patinkin, M. (1989) Fast heat: How Korea won the microwave war. *Harvard Business Review*, **67**, 1, 83–92.
8. Bartlett, C. and Ghoshal, S. (1989) *Managing Across Borders: The Transnational Solution*. Boston, MA: Harvard University Press.
9. Prahalad, C. K. and Hamel, G. (1990) The core competence of the corporation. *Harvard Business Review*, **90**, 3, 79–91.
10. Zuboff, S. (1988) *In the Age of the Smart Machine*. Oxford: Heinemann.
11. Venkatraman, N. (1991) IT-induced business reconfiguration. In M. S. Scott Morton (ed.) *The Corporation of the 1990s*. New York: Oxford University Press.
12. Bamber, G. J. and Whitehouse, G. (1992) International data on economic, employment and human resource issues. *International Journal of Human Resource Management*, **3**, 2, 347–370.

Chapter Six

UK LIMITED

SHORT-TERMISM

Taking a global perspective from the general's HQ is challenging enough. Taking a national one must make our captains of industry feel that they are fighting with cavalry against cannon. Or, to get away from the incessant military metaphors of business language, that their own goalposts are wider than those of their competitors.

The captains of UK industry see this country as their base for engaging the global market. For many more senior executives, it is not only their base but their main market as well. What options does the UK offer? What opportunities and constraints do the financial, political and social institutions of our nation provide? We will argue in this chapter that they lead executives inexorably towards one strategy only—to cut costs and improve productivity.

Consider first the financial structures within which they have to operate. How ironic that the very pension funds on which managers have relied to keep them in the style to which they are accustomed when they retire are one of the main reasons for the early shattering of these same retirement dreams[1]. Shareholders are mostly (in terms of volume) investors of pension funds or corporate moneys. Their main concern is to maintain as high a rate of immediate shareholder benefit as possible. The half-yearly accounts are also treated as the key index of vulnerability to takeover. They are pored over "by a horde of analysts, pontificating on their share price and concerned solely with short-term share performance rather than long-term growth and investment"[2]. Share price and corporate survival are therefore intimately connected. With the rules regarding takeover so lax in the UK, takeover bids can be talked up by analysts, hatched in private, and then sprung suddenly. So the moral is: the immediate bottom line is always the top priority.

LACK OF SUPPORT

With the Treasury and the Bank of England vying with each other in their ideological zeal to control inflation as their only legitimate involvement, any central help with investment is politically verboten. What a contrast with the example of Samsung (Chapter Five), where the Korean Economic Development Board provided tax rebates for export and made low-cost loans for investment in selected new products[3].

The lending banks, too, are feeling vulnerable. Instead of forging long-term investment relationships with organizations as in, for example, Germany and Japan, the UK banks have distanced themselves from industry. With bad debts of £2 billion in 1992/3, for example, the National Westminster Bank, having invested extensively in the Third World, has retrenched domestically too. Lending is under tight central control, and both large and small corporate borrowers have to present only low-risk propositions for investment. So the necessary support for innovation in terms of investment capital simply isn't forthcoming.

FICTITIOUS CAPITAL

Major changes have overtaken the City as a whole. With the deregulation of the finance industry and the internationalization of banking, the City has become open to international competition[4]. With New York nine times as large as the City and Tokyo three times as large, it has recently concentrated on circulating capital internationally. Its prime concern now is with money dealing and interest-bearing capital. Its deals are in stocks and shares, national bonds, and interbank bonds with other financial centres. It is concerned less and less with financing British industry. It deals more in fictitious capital than in real business[5].

So neither fund managers, banks, nor government appear interested in investing in the longer-term development of our industry. On the contrary, more than any other nation, our financial institutions impose short-term perspectives upon the captains of industry. Some, like Unilever, have built upon a long history of global operations and avoided this short-termism. Others, like Grand Metropolitan, have developed brand success internationally. But for most, there has seemed no alternative: they feel they have to attempt to achieve a competitive advantage by cost cutting, productivity and tight budgetary control.

BACK TO BASICS OR START AGAIN

It's instructive to look at these strategic reactions in terms of the well-known analysis of Miles and Snow[6]. They distinguished:

- Reactors—organizations which simply react to environmental change in order to survive. Typically, they bring in a new top team and employ a cheaper labour force.
- Defenders, who aim to retain or enhance their share of one particular market.
- Analysers, who aim to build on market share in core areas by carefully researching and moving into others.
- Prospectors, who look to move rapidly into or out of markets.

The general picture most recently has been a set of shifts back towards Defender and Reactor mode. Traditional Analysers such as ICI have sought to concentrate on core businesses within two separate organizations[7]. Prospectors like BTR and Hanson have sold off their more peripheral acquisitions and exercised ever tighter budgetary control over their remaining satellites. Control of costs by stripping away non-core business elements and contracting out internal functions has been the order of the day.

Where there has been a move towards innovation and new markets is in the establishment of new small enterprises. Instead of feeling able to allow their experts some autonomy and decentralized units, captains of industry fume as their innovative people leave to set up on their own. In 1991, firms employing fewer than ten people accounted for 35 per cent of all non-governmental employment. When we consider firms of fewer than 50 we are talking of 99 per cent of all businesses and 42 per cent of employment. While mortality of small businesses is high, their birthrate is even higher.

HISTORY ANCIENT AND MODERN

There are yet more factors which predispose towards a cost-cutting, productivity- improving strategy. The decentralization of industrial relations bargaining so that negotiations are at plant level allows local management to relate pay to productivity[8]. Reward can now be performance-related, thereby, in theory, improving productivity. Central financial control over these local budgets can prevent costs escalating. Thus the recent decreased power of the unions has permitted methods aimed at boosting productivity.

However, the longer-term history of the British industrial structure is probably the most powerful constraint on strategic choice[9]. UK organizations tend to be older, since we were the first into the industrial revolution. Older organizations developed in stable markets and therefore became bureaucratic in structure[10]. Bureaucratic structures are good for controlling behaviour and expenditure, so the mechanisms appropriate for retrenchment are often already in place. Others, such as performance-related pay, have recently been introduced. Allied to the tendency to centralize decision-making when recession strikes, these structural factors render cost control a much more likely proposition than innovation into new products and markets.

SKILLS SHORTFALL

Anyway, innovation requires a different set of conditions. It needs, according to Porter[11] a highly educated workforce, advanced technology, a sophisticated home market and internal competition. Only if these factors are present can innovation occur on a national scale. We can see pockets of excellence in the UK where these conditions apply: pharmaceuticals, for example, and films and television programmes.

Overall, however, our captains of industry despair at the educational level of their workforce. True, in the last five years, the annual production of graduates has increased from 15 to 30 per cent of those entering the workforce. Yet this has been achieved with minimal increase in resources to universities, and the consequent risk of reduced teaching standards. Moreover, the majority of the added graduates are in arts or social science, not in science or engineering. As a consequence it is students with the lowest entry qualifications who are entering the disciplines regarded as most crucial to product innovation. Regardless of the quality of graduate output, 80 per cent of the UK workforce for the year AD2000 has already left full-time education; the effects of these educational advances take long periods to work through. In the meantime, some of the Tiger economies put 75 per cent through higher education already. Other international comparisons are equally unflattering. In terms of the 16 year olds reaching the equivalent of GCSE grades A–C in mathematics, native language and one science, the percentages in 1990–91 were as follows: France 66; Germany 62; Japan 50; England 27. In terms of full-time participation in education or training by 16–18 year olds, the picture is as gloomy: some 40 per cent in the UK in 1990, compared with 88 per cent in Germany. If the projections to the year 2000 are correct[12], we will be needing more managers and professionals who need not only their initial formation but also continuous subsequent lifelong development. The educational expansion has been underfunded, too little, and too late.

So everything about the UK points to a preference for a cost-cutting strategy:

♦ The short-term perspective of finance
♦ The lack of investment in industry

- The decline in power of the unions
- The age and bureaucratic structure of many companies
- The shortage of knowledge and skills

The recent actions of executives become more comprehensible when we see them from the global and the national perspectives which they themselves are forced to take.

REFERENCES

1. Hutton, W. (1994) Bad times for the good life. *The Guardian*, August 2nd.
2. Beresford, P. (1992) Selling the UK short. *Management Today*, May, p. 3.
3. Magaziner, I. C. and Patinkin, M. (1989) Fast heat: How Korea won the microwave war. *Harvard Business Review*, **67**, 1, 83–92.
4. Hilton, A. (1987). *City within a State: A Portrait of Britain's Financial World.* London: IB Tauris.
5. Moorhouse, H. F. (1989) No mean city? The financial sector and the decline of manufacturing in Britain. *Work, Employment and Society*, **3**, 1, 105–118.
6. Miles, R. E. and Snow, C. C. (1978) *Organizational Structure, Strategy and Process.* New York: McGraw-Hill.
7. Donaldson, H. (1994) Under the microscope: Personnel's role in a demerger. *Personnel Management*, **26**, 2, 34–38.
8. Purcell, J. (1989) Managing decentralized bargaining. *Personnel Management*, **21**, 5, 53–57.
9. Begin, J. P. (1992) Comparative human resource management (HRM): a systems perspective. *International Journal of Human Resource Management*, **3**, 3, 379–408.
10. Baird, L. and Meshoulam, I. (1988) Managing two fits of strategic human resource management. *Academy of Management Review*, **13**, 1, 116–128.
11. Porter, M. E. (1990) *The Competitive Advantage of Nations.* New York: The Free Press.
12. University of Warwick Industrial Relations Research Unit. *Patterns of Employment.* University of Warwick, 1993.

Chapter Seven

FRIENDS, FADS AND FIXES

CULTURES AND CONTACTS

Global and national competition, demanding shareholders, menacing conglomerates—where are the captains of industry to turn for help? They turn to their Boards; to networks of contacts at the same level as themselves[1, 2]; and to consultants. They go, in other words, to people like themselves; and to people who claim to offer solutions. We will argue in this chapter that the specific practices of the last decade are consequential upon these sources of advice. Once cost-competitiveness and productivity appear the only feasible strategic objectives, then the methods for achieving them are a matter of top people's culture and contacts.

The composition of Boards of Directors tends to reflect national business values. Financial people are well represented on most boards, reflecting the importance placed on the bottom line in UK industry. Look at the photos in the UK business press, and that dynamic duo the Chief Executive and the Finance Director are likely to feature. Look at their German counterparts, and you're likely to see an engineer rather than an accountant. Moreover, British boards are mostly highly homogeneous in their composition[3]. Board members tend to come from the same background as each other, and are more often than not home-grown by the organization[4]. Even the non-executive directors are often former executive directors of the firm, or are chosen for their compatibility with the Board.

Not many directors are in close touch with employees at all levels of the organization. Rather, they construe their task as that of operating at the strategic level. So we have a set of people responding strategically to the business environment who are very like each other and who are often insulated from other employees. It is hardly surprising that many such groups share a culture: a set of assumptions, values and artefacts.

Among the assumptions that are common in Anglo-American business circles is the assumption that *employees* are human capital. They are costs when they are non-productive and assets when they are productive. Either way, they are there to enable business objectives to be met; they are human resources. Moreover, while management writers come up with a wide variety of metaphors for *organizations*, senior managers generally seem to be happiest with notions of machine or structure. As a consequence of these two assumptions, senior business people sometimes form very instrumental plans for action. They seem to believe that if you pull certain levers (organization = machine), people will respond in certain ways (person = asset to be acted upon).

THE SEARCH FOR LEVERS

The various HR initiatives of the last decade are these intended levers. A clear causal relationship is expected between the pulling of a lever and a change in behaviour: e.g. the introduction of performance-related pay will produce more accountability and effort and hence greater individual productivity. It is the shared *assumptions* which suggest that there are levers which could work. It is the shared *contacts* which determine which levers are chosen.

It is easy to dismiss the various HR systems and techniques of the present and the recent past as mere fads, or fashions. But this is really only a description, not an explanation. All it tells us is that a particular technique is used by several companies for a period, then is abandoned (although elements may be retained and incorporated). We need to ask why this happens[6]. Here are some possible reasons:

1. The possibility of missing out on a source of competitive advantage. A technique may seem way-out, without rationale, but if X is doing it, it must be worth trying.
2. The need to appear to customers and to competitors to be at the cutting edge—to be doing the very latest thing.
3. The feeling that one can't afford to be seen not to use a particular technique, since most others are already doing so.
4. The need, particularly for HR directors, to be seen to be *doing something* in the present predicament.
5. The difficulty of choosing from a multitude of alternatives being offered, and the consequent decision to make responsibility collective by going for what the others are choosing.
6. Trusting in a guru's solutions for the same reason; i.e. in this case, putting the responsibility onto an "expert" rather than onto other organizations.
7. Being sucked in to the product cycle of consultancy firms. This cycle normally requires a shelf-life of 2 or 3 years per product. Where the product is transparent and rational, other consultants will soon provide it cheaper, or firms will do it for themselves. Where it is opaque and requires unique expertise, some firms will be tied in for longer while others will denounce it as mumbo-jumbo.
8. Lacking a model of organization and of behaviour, and therefore keeping all one's options open. Anything might work—we've no means of knowing until we (or preferably someone else) has tried it out (Anglo-Saxon empiricism).
9. Being influenced, as a consequence, by a consistent set of anecdotes purveyed by consultants of successful applications in similar organizations.

Readers may care to apply the above set of explanations to their own experience of any of the following:

- empowerment
- outsourcing
- business process re-engineering
- performance-related pay
- neuro-linguistic programming
- total quality management
- quality circles
- quality certification (ISO, BS)
- managerial competencies
- corporate culture change
- annual hours
- charismatic leadership
- management grid
- new age training
- the learning organization
- action learning

You may not be aware of the processes whereby this or that fad became adopted in your own organization. If our analysis above is correct, however, they were likely to include:

♦ Getting information from contacts about competitors' practices.
♦ Getting information from contacts about their own practices.
♦ Benchmarking one's own current practices against those of so-called excellent companies.
♦ Attending presentations by consultants.
♦ Consulting contacts about their experience of different consultants.

THE MARKETING OF A PRODUCT

Consider one of the latest products, *business process re-engineering* (BPR) by way of example[7]. As usual, the concept and the product came from the USA. Nowhere in the world are there more concepts and products, promoted by more consultants, to more hungry and open-minded executives. BPR had the usual promotion strategy:

1. Invent a title for a product which implies that it's new. (There is little new under the sun. BPR incorporates many ideas and practices about the organization of work, some of which date back as far as scientific management days.)
2. Make sure the title implies that executives can do something visible and radical which has an effect: a top-down revolution.
3. Introduce it as a root and branch remedy for the now recognized ineffectiveness of previously fashionable techniques. ("They were mere tinkerings: this is an all-or-nothing proposition with an uncertain result.")
4. Give it thereby the glamour of being an heroic risk. ("This is a bet-the-business proposition. You have to reinvent yourselves from scratch.")
5. Gain respectability by publishing the idea in the *Harvard Business Review*[8], then writing a book[9].
6. Gain credibility by quoting companies which have been converted to the idea; keep quiet about failures, fees and follies.
7. Move on before the inevitable backlash sets in, and before serious and impartial investigators fail to discover universal benefits.
8. Continue to market the product across the world where the truth has not yet dawned and where the natives still need missionaries. ("In Europe these ideas have not, as yet, been extensively communicated. There are fewer organizations active in this area. Some cultures are more receptive than others. I predict that Britain will eventually do well with these notions.")[10]

Business process re-engineering has been singled out for analysis only because it is a recent example of the genre. A similar analysis could have been made of most of the other techniques of the last decade. Nor is BPR any less likely to meet organizations' immediate concerns than the others. On the contrary, because, when practised properly, it forces people to think carefully about how they do important things, it may well prove beneficial to some organizations. We have chosen it because it perfectly exemplifies the methods used to popularize and sell the latest fad. In making these comments we are differentiating between consultancy as the selling of a highly priced product, and consultancy as a high-value, highly skilled service. Good consultancy is about helping clients discover and solve their own problems, it's not about universal solutions.

In Chapters Five and Six, we sought to understand the competitive pressures forcing down upon senior executives, and their impatience with the UK as a base to fight from. In this context, the aims of cutting costs and increasing productivity are entirely comprehensible. In this chapter, we have looked at the social contacts, the shared assumptions and the product marketing which have led them towards the supposed solutions of the last decade. The desperation of the middle managers at the receiving end of these "solutions" is only matched by that of the senior executives who grab at straws in the face of overwhelming competitive turmoil. It remains to discuss what have been the outcomes of these interventions.

REFERENCES

1. Hales, C. P. (1986) What do managers do? A critical review of the evidence. *Journal of Management Studies*, **23**, 88–115.
2. Kotter, J. P. (1982) *The General Managers*. New York: The Free Press.
3. Herriot, P. and Pemberton, C. (1995) *Competitive Advantage through Diversity*. London: Sage.
4. Hambrick, D. C. and Mason, P. A. (1984) Upper echelons: The organization as a reflexion of its top managers. *Academy of Management Review*, **9**, 2, 193–196.
5. Morgan, G. (1986) *Images of Organization*. California: Sage.
6. Huczynski, A. A. (1993) Explaining the succession of management fads. *International Journal of Human Resource Management*, **4**, 2, 443–464.
7. Thackray, J. (1993) Fads, fixes and fictions. *Management Today*, June, 40–43.
8. Hammer, M. (1990) Reengineering work: Don't automate, obliterate. *Harvard Business Review*, **68**, 4, 104–112.
9. Hammer, M. and Champy, J. (1993) *Reengineering the Corporation*. London: Nicholas Brealey.
10. Ibid., p. 106.

Chapter Eight

BLOOD, TOIL, SWEAT AND TEARS—FOR WHAT?

WHAT ARE ORGANIZATIONS?

Have they worked? Have all the sacrifices and upheavals been worthwhile? Have costs been cut and productivity improved? Has competitiveness sharpened and survival been secured? Both those on the imposing and those on the receiving end would love to know the answers to these questions. Unfortunately, they are incredibly difficult to ascertain.

Why? The question seems pretty straightforward. Has it worked or hasn't it? It's not so simple. First, we need to explore the assumptions underlying the question. They are the assumptions common to the Anglo-Saxon business cultures: you can do something to an organization which will have the desired effect. You can pull a lever and obtain a response. There is a clear, single, linear cause–effect relationship.

Underlying these assumptions is a mental model of organization as machine. Yet, as we knew decades ago[1], and as we keep being reminded[2], organizations are better theorized as open systems. Interventions are likely to have multiple interacting consequences, some of which may be unforeseeable to even the wisest consultant. "A butterfly fluttering its wings in Beijing", etc., etc. To use the old stone in the pond analogy, as we have elsewhere[3], one can cast yet another fad into the organizational pool. The waves it makes will instantly meet the waves from previous fads, many of which will have hit the banks and bounced back. You certainly can't tell which waves were made by which fad, especially since the whole pond is heaving with the consequences of two other events totally outside your control: a harsh wind has got up, originating in the Far East; and an interloper has even dared to launch his boat out onto your pond.

Organizations are complex open systems. Many of them face similar problems in their environment, but it doesn't follow that they all need the same solutions. For too long, the captains of industry have laboured under the burdens of "best practice" and "benchmarking". These concepts are underpinned by the same assumption: that there are sophisticated state-of-the-art levers which work in any organization. It cannot be said often enough—organizations differ by technology, sector, structure, size, age, history, market and people[4]. Their HR and business strategies develop as part of the changes in these internal and external features[5].

To take a specific example, it's quite apparent why "best practice" isn't scattered at random across industries. Rather, many of the most sophisticated practices in the area of training and development were to be found in the computer industry—IBM, Hewlett-Packard, Digital, Wang, Apple, etc. This is because the rapid technological change, need for diagnostic production skills and the predominance of professionals in the workforce required people development; and the continuous growth which had been typical ensured employment security and resources. All organizations played their part in developing a well-trained innovative industry-wide workforce. How different today—they are, many of them, in the labour market for people trained by their competitors. Investment in development at the industry level is fine; at the organizational level it's another matter when a competitor is likely to reap the benefit from your investment. So "best practice" varies according to sector; there's no one right way.

WHO ARE PEOPLE?

The question "has it worked?" not only begs some assumptions about the model of *organizations*, though. It also raises issues about the model of *people* that underlies the question. In particular, it raises issues about the nature of the relationship between organizations and employees. A human capital model of people implies organizational assets whose purpose is to achieve business objectives. Assets are there to be manipulated, put to best use, invested, expended. In sum, assets have things done to them. The relationship implies exploitation (not necessarily in its pejorative sense) by one party of the other. Ultimately, however, the employment relationship is one of exchange: the psychological contract. True, an imbalance of power in favour of one of the parties is likely to make the contract appear inequitable; but however unfair the deal appears, the relationship implies mutual promises and obligations. It also allows for differing interests[6].

These are not mere philosophical musings. They have a profound effect upon outcomes. Indeed, we will argue that many of the recent fads have not fulfilled their extravagant manifestos because they are premised on inappropriate models of organizations and people. The specific objectives of the supposed pull on the lever may or may not have been achieved, but the overall balance of all its consequences— serendipitous benefits and unforeseen costs— is what matters. And people don't simply change their behaviour when acted upon, like Pavlov's dogs or Skinner's rats. There are complex intervening mental processes, many of which involve hostility to the experience of having no say in their own manipulation. In general, such organizationally important mental processes as commitment cannot be engineered. Rather, they are a consequence of a relationship in which parties honour promises, perceive equity, and respect and trust each other.

So the question with which we started this chapter—"Have they worked?"—has turned into the question "What have their consequences been?" At the most basic level, for example, we can ask not only "Has downsizing cut costs?" but also "has it improved productivity?" And, even if the answer to both these questions is yes, we may still find, for example, that quality has suffered. On the other hand, it will be extremely difficult to attribute any of these outcomes to the downsizing alone, since a range of other contemporary interventions or events may have been responsible, too.

RECENT EVIDENCE

When we look at the impartial investigations of some of the fads, though, a picture begins to emerge. Where the overall balance of outcomes has been judged unfavourable, this is either because the complexity of organizations was ignored and unintended consequences were not foreseen; or it is because people have been regarded as objects to be manipulated rather than as individuals to be contracted with and respected.

It is worth treating one fad at length in order to support these assertions; but it's clear that in general the management press is beginning to be appropriately sceptical about gurus and their fads. Here are a few recent titles:

♦ "Fads, Fixes and Fictions" (about BPR)
♦ "The Trouble with PRP"
♦ "The Case against Decentralized Pay"
♦ "Annual hours: a year of living dangerously"
♦ "Waving or drowning in participation?"
♦ "Decentralizing pay decisions: empowerment or abdication?"
♦ "Exploding the myth of greenfield sites"
♦ "Empowerment: spinach of the 90s or flavour of the month?"
♦ "Does lean necessarily equal mean?"
♦ "Who needs a hero?"
♦ "Why empowerment is a con".

However, neither tides of opinion nor anecdotes from gurus or converts are any substitute for disinterested empirical research. Two recent studies have, for example, examined performance-related pay (PRP); one by NEDO/Institute of Personnel Management, and the other by the Institute of Manpower Studies[7]. The overt objective of PRP is to motivate people to become more productive by making a certain proportion of their salary contingent upon their meeting their performance objectives. Responses of employees in anonymous questionnaires indicated that:

♦ PRP conflicted with effective teamworking
♦ The system was not perceived as fair—pay didn't reflect performance
♦ The objectives changed too often or not often enough
♦ The rules intended to ensure equity resulted in "games-playing"
♦ Managers weren't skilled enough at appraisal, either in setting targets or in assessing performance
♦ Pay is not an effective motivator for all

What is clear from these results is that there were a variety of outcomes other than those expected; organizations are complicated social systems in which individuals do not operate in isolation. Second, where new systems involving reward are imposed, considerations of equity will be paramount in the minds of many. Perceptions of inequity may well negate any direct motivational effect of reward. Third, where employees are treated as human capital, their individual differences will be ignored; some will not want more money, yet they have had no say in striking the new bargain when exchanging performance for financial reward.

Many other interventions which have been investigated impartially arrive at the same sorts of conclusion. This is especially true of those programmes designed to increase commitment to the organization, and thence, indirectly, productivity. Culture change programmes for example, seldom work when imposed from above[8]. Do as I say *and* do as I do isn't always the message received down the line. Recent research[9] suggests that commitment is generally consequent upon perceived equity of policies and good career opportunities. Given that many interventions are perceived to be inequitable; and given that downsizing and delayering have reduced career opportunities; then commitment to the organization is likely to have been one of the first casualties. We are left with the conclusion that the increased productivity evidenced during the last decade is a result of fewer people working longer hours, in order to earn their right to continued employment.

From the perspective of the captains of industry, this may not matter too much. What they are grateful for is that their organizations have survived both the competitive bloodbath and one of the two worst recessions of the century. They believe they have done so by cutting costs and persuading the markets that they are more efficient. What they may not realize is that in so doing they have set in motion a revolution in the nature of the employment relationship the like of which they never imagined. For they have shattered the old psychological contract and failed to negotiate a new one.

REFERENCES

1. Katz, R. and Kahn, D. (1978) *The Social Psychology of Organizations* (2nd edn). New York: John Wiley.
2. Senge, P. (1990) *The Fifth Discipline*. New York: Doubleday.
3. Herriot, P. and Pemberton, C. (1995) *Competitive Advantage through Diversity*. London: Sage.
4. Storey, J. (1993) The take-up of human resource management by mainstream companies: key lessons from research. *International Journal of Human Resource Management*, **4**, 3, 529–553.
5. Purcell, J. (1993) The challenge of human resource management for industrial relations research and practice. *International Journal of Human Resource Management*, **4**, 3, 511–527.
6. Keenoy, T. (1990) HRM: A case of the wolf in sheep's clothing? *Personnel Review*, **19**, 2, 3–9.
7. Robinson, S. (1992) The trouble with PRP. *Human Resources*, **5**, 66–72.
8. Beer, M., Eisenstat, R. A. and Spector, B. (1990) Why change programmes don't produce change. *Harvard Business Review*, **68**, 6, 158–166.
9. Morris, T., Lydka, H. and O'Greevy, M. F. (1993) Can commitment be managed? A longitudinal analysis of employee commitment and human resource policies. *Human Resource Management Journal*, **3**, 3, 21–42.

Part Three

THE REAL IMPACT

Chapter Nine

IT CAN'T HAPPEN TO ME

THE REVOLUTION ISN'T OVER YET

One reaction to our book so far could be: what more is there to say? The old psychological contract has gone, there's a new one in its place, and once people get used to it things will settle down and get back to normal. The revolution has happened: long live the new regime.

Wishful thinking! The revolution is only part-way through (and so is the book). The present psychological contract consists of longer hours, harder work, broader skills and tolerance of change in exchange for high pay and the privilege of having a job at all. This contract can't last. It's merely a transition point, a way-stage towards a much more complex picture.

Why are we so confident? There are several reasons why employment relations cannot remain as they are:

1. Many managers have not yet come to terms with the fact that the old contract no longer operates. While they appreciate that it has

61

gone for good, they have not yet understood its implications for them personally. A new page has not yet been started—the previous page is still being turned over.

2. The profundity of the effects of the loss of the old contract and the imposition of the new has not yet been appreciated. Managers and professionals do not merely feel angry or insecure; rather, their feelings of equity and trust have been violated, and their very identity threatened. The consequence is that the main objective of the change—to increase productivity—is threatened. If you've been mugged once, you don't lay yourself open to being taken advantage of again. No amount of careful management of the mugging process will persuade you otherwise.

3. Business imperatives will dictate a further phase of the revolution in the psychological contract. The present contract supports a business strategy of survival through cost-competitiveness. Yet this will not ensure survival in the future. Cost-competitiveness will cease to be in itself a source of competitive advantage: it will be a given, a taken-for-granted quality of every organization. Innovative products and services faster to market will be the new key to survival and prosperity. And if there is one thing the present psychological contract is guaranteed not to produce, it's innovation. Who can be innovative when they are totally exhausted and continuously constrained by the bottom line? Who will take risks when to do so lays you open to dismissal?

THEY UNDERSTAND THE CONTEXT

First, then, we argue that the first page hasn't yet been turned over. Many managers appreciate the general business situation, but still fail to apply its lessons to their own careers.

In terms of their understanding of the business scene, managers are only too clear. Here are the percentages of a sample of members of the Institute of Management agreeing with the following statements:[1]:

♦ Environmental and social pressures are increasing   98%
♦ Customers are becoming more demanding   97%

- ◆ The rate of change is speeding up   92%
- ◆ More markets are becoming global   91%
- ◆ Markets are becoming more open and competitive   83%

They also recognize the structural changes that the need to be cost-competitive has produced. In our own survey of 1646 managers in the finance sector[2]:

- ◆ 65 per cent agreed that their organization was facing a battle to survive
- ◆ 63 per cent agreed that the number of managerial levels would continue to decrease
- ◆ 51 per cent disagreed that the size of the workforce would stabilize, with a further 28 per cent feeling neutral

Many of our respondents recognized the underlying causes, too:

> The clients, our policy-holders, and staff appear to play second fiddle to shareholders whose only aim is increased growth or dividends. The loss of experienced managerial and non-managerial staff in our organization will have, in my opinion, a detrimental long-term effect on our business in pursuit of short-term savings. Accountants are taking over our industry, which is increasingly being run at the top level by people who know little or nothing about our industry, let alone our organization.

BUT IT CAN'T HAPPEN TO ME

Yet despite their appreciation of what's going on, there's still evidence among managers of the "it can't happen to me" syndrome. For example, from our sample, 55 per cent thought it unlikely that they would be made redundant[2]. In 1992, 82 per cent of middle managers were aware of downsizing and delayering, but 79 per cent reported that restructuring wasn't a threat to their current job and 64 per cent regarded it as something that wasn't going to affect their management career in general. Fully 73 per cent saw the rest of their career as consisting of a managerial role within an organization[3].

A year later, a sample from the same population of managers was slightly less optimistic[4]. This time 36 per cent, as opposed to 54 per cent, thought their next move would be upward. Expectation of a sideways move remained constant at 14 per cent, and only 6 per cent expected redundancy; yet the current evidence indicates that about one third of managers have experienced redundancy. An amazing 36 per cent still believed, in 1993, that they would stay with their present organization till retirement; yet 86 per cent of them were under 55 years old, 40 per cent under 45.

THE EXPECTATION LAG AND WHAT IT IMPLIES

The picture is one of a slow change in managers' attitudes and expectations for their own careers, a change which lags far behind the events themselves. This is why, as redundancies and delayerings continue through the 90s, some of the managers affected will continue to be surprised, shocked and devastated. It's why the final page of the old contract has yet to be turned.

Why are people so irrational? Why can't they see it could happen to them and prepare for it? The answer is easy, and doesn't assume irrationality. They have their reasons, but these are derived from their personal experience and not from their scanning of their environment. Suppose I am a middle manager, who has been regularly promoted throughout my career, favourably appraised and recently rewarded with a performance-based bonus. Being human, I will attribute these events to my own worth[5]. Being British and Anglo-Saxon, I'll only trust the evidence of my own experience[6]. Either way, I'm not going to believe it's going to happen to me until it does. Or else, if I see it happening to people just like me, I may construe it as a possibility.

The implication of these findings for organizations is considerable. They cannot assume a ready acceptance that the present deal exists just because they have imposed it. Rather, they have to continue to expect the same hostile reactions whenever the terms of the old deal are broken. After all, the psychological contract is intensely personal in the mind of the employee. It involves an individual deal, based on all the investments and sacrifices *I've* made. Surely they can't ignore all that. Surely it counts for something. They can, and it doesn't.

REFERENCES

1. Coulson-Thomas, C. and Coe, T. (1991) *The Flat Organization: Philosophy and Practice.* Corby: British Institute of Management.
2. Herriot, P., Pemberton, C. and Hawtin, E. (1995) The career attitudes and intentions of managers in the UK finance sector. *British Journal of Management* (in press).
3. Wheatley, M. (1992). *The Future of Middle Management.* Corby: British Institute of Management.
4. Coe, T. (1993) *Managers under Stress.* Corby: Institute of Management.
5. Weiner, B., Frieze, I. H., Kukla, A., Reed, L., Rest, S. and Rosenbaum, R. M. (1971) *Perceiving the Causes of Success and Failure.* Morristown, NJ: General Learning Press.
6. Hofstede, G. (1991) *Cultures and Organizations: Software of the Mind.* Maidenhead: McGraw-Hill.

Chapter Ten

FAIRNESS AND RESPECT

EXPECTATIONS, EQUITY AND MORE

One organizational reaction to the time lag between events and adjusted expectations is to seek to manage these expectations. How can we hasten managers' perception that jobs aren't for life and that the old contract's gone? How can we so manage the process of redundancy as to make things easier for those who leave and for those who remain? How can we subsequently manage the feelings of those who remain so that they will accept the present psychological contract and be highly motivated to achieve their side of that bargain?

These are the obvious questions to ask; but they are the wrong ones. We argue that the consequences of the violation of the old contract and the imposition of the present one are so profound that they cannot be "managed away". The only path open to organizations is to move through to new forms of psychological contract which meet both their own and their employees' needs and preferences. Careful management of the whole process of restructuring is certainly necessary. But it is not sufficient for longer-term survival.

The effects on those who are made redundant and on those who remain have been likened to the effects of bereavement[1,2]. The point that's being made is that the loss of job or of colleagues is a profound one. The violation of the old contract and its unilateral replacement by the present one affect people to the root of their being.

First, people perceive *inequity*, both in the outcomes themselves and in the way they were carried through. Second, because of such inequity and the violation of the old contract, people lose whatever *trust* they once had in their employing organization. Third, because of the imposition of the present contract, people start to feel *powerless* to affect what happens to them. Finally, they feel depersonalized and worthless as their very *identity* is threatened.

These may appear alarmist assertions. Listen carefully to what middle managers are saying and you will realize that they actually are necessary to do justice to the depth of their feelings. We will start nearest the surface with their feelings of *inequity*. Feelings of inequity are more likely in cultures such as the UK and the USA, where individual performance and its rewards are emphasized[3]. Where individuals have invested a lot, and where they currently perform well, just rewards are expected.

UNFAIR OUTCOMES AND THEIR JUSTIFICATION

Here is the reaction to the redundancy of a young achiever whose performance clearly merited retention and reward[4].

> There was a guy who had master-minded and written a brilliant client proposal and won a large contract in a very difficult competitive situation. He was at that time the best thing since sliced bread and earned a very fat bonus. Within four months he was made redundant. It reverberated around the corridors, because it was so unjust. There were no hidden reasons, they were thinning out his division and just picked on him. They left behind people who were nowhere near his calibre. (He has since done very well

as an independent consultant on his own.) His name must have been put on a list without any consideration to merit, and passed upstairs. The MD should have queried it, but he did not do so. It was totally illogical to have selected that man for redundancy.

In the USA, it's primarily present performance which decides whether others think that a redundancy is fair, although length of time in the firm and the commitments of long-term employment the organization has made are also factors which people take into account[5]. What particularly riles is when top people receive huge payoffs, or when they engineer their own survival. For example:

> *****, like most other financial institutions, has gone through and continues to go through rapid change. Not a bad thing. In my view, the senior management (general manager and assistant general manager level) is like a "men's club", with people trying to protect themselves and their teams.

Contrast the case where the directors of a small firm actually took a cut in their salaries— and note the consequences[4]!

> I work for a small family bakery business with a staff of just seven. It is presently having a hard time and is struggling to avoid becoming one of the statistics that make up the long list of business failures. We have recently lost our two best contract customers. The net effect in reduced profits means that the two owners take home less money than I do. Staff loyalty has really surfaced in our present predicament. They have taken the initiative and said to the owners that they do not expect salary increases this year. They have also suggested several significant cost-saving measures. The owners would undoubtedly have announced a salary standstill, but it was a very nice gesture for the staff to volunteer it first. The staff are determined to help the business survive; I count their motive as loyalty (not self-interest) because most could easily find another job.

Of course, organizations invent all sorts of explanations to assuage these feelings of inequity. In place of people's general sense of fairness in social exchange, they substitute a variety of alternatives[6]. Some are *ideological*:

- In a free market economy, it's the leanest and fittest organizations which survive.
- In a free labour market, exactly the same thing happens. The weakest will go to the wall, and this is beneficial in the long run.

Other justifications are through *comparisons*. Just as employees compare their redundancy settlements with the golden handshakes of directors, so organizations seek to introduce different reference groups:

- Others have been sacked at a moment's notice—at least you're getting outplacement.
- This current downsizing is the biggest and worst; anything subsequent that those who remain will suffer is minor by comparison.

Still other justifications can be excuses or *disclaimers* put out prior to the event:

- The big shareholders are putting pressure on us to raise dividends at year end.
- We're having to outsource a lot of the work to Taiwan.

Some of these justifications may have a sound basis. The real question is: to what extent are they likely to be believed? Only if they are believed will they assuage feelings of injustice. Yet a key variable for the persuasive power of communications is the credibility of their source[7]. And in this case, top management have often lost their credibility by behaving in unfair ways themselves. Apart from the huge payoffs to directors who leave, the salaries of those who remain have increased more than those of everyone else in percentage terms[8]. In the last five years, salaries of executives have risen by 77 per cent, while average wages have risen by 17 per cent.

UNFAIR PROCESS: THE LAST STRAW

Even stronger feelings of injustice arise not from *what* was done, but from *how* it was done. How exactly were the decisions taken, and how were people dealt with when the blow fell? Some research[9] suggests that when the *process* is managed well, the *outcomes* may not be seen as nearly so unfair as when the process is itself unfair. What's more, these effects occur more powerfully for those who had a high prior commitment to the organization[10]. If you've really committed yourself to your employer, then you're going to be extremely angry if they don't take care *how* they deal with you.

People want to have some say in how decisions are to be taken—perhaps out of self-interest, or perhaps just so that they can affirm themselves by expressing their values[11]. They want to receive, or see others receiving:

♦ Appropriate support and compensation in redundancy.
♦ Fair criteria for selection for redundancy, applied consistently and without bias.
♦ Accurate and advance information.
♦ The possibility of appeal or correction of a decision.
♦ To be represented when the decision is taken[12].

They want dignity and respect in how people are treated[13] and they *don't* want top management bad-mouthing those gone ("Now we've got rid of the dead wood, we can start motoring"). On the contrary, the survivors like to hear how many of their redundant colleagues have found new jobs after outplacement[14].

Yet what actually happens? Let people speak for themselves:

♦ They've changed the rules of the game![4]

> When I joined ***** twenty-odd years ago, salary grading and selection for promotion were very substantially dependent on job experience, seniority, loyalty and endeavour, those sort of qualities. Now it is excessively weighted towards paper qualifications. There has been no official policy dictate about this. The change has been gradual but cumulative. It has left long service people like myself at a permanent disadvantage compared to the more recent entrants. I judge our contribution to be equal to if not greater than theirs.

♦ It falls like a bolt from the blue[4]

I think that one of our managers was treated abominably when he was summarily sacked without just cause. As you know, there has been a lot of rationalization in ***** since the stock market crash last October. We have merged with two other firms because of the fall in trading turnover. This man worked his guts out to fit the three lots of staff together, and to merge the client list, etc. He had been highly commended, and hints had been dropped that he was in line for a big promotion. This particular day in question, ***** was called into the director's office. He straightened his tie, dusted his shoulders, wiped his shoes up the back of his trouser legs, etc. and in he went. He thought this is it! And it was! When he came back, he looked terrible. He phoned his wife and she was crying, his secretary was crying and in the end we were all crying. It was like receiving news of a sudden death in the family. He said "The decision is made, nothing in this world will change it now."

♦ It can be made with gross insensitivity[4]

One incident that happened in one of our many reorganizations that made staff feel badly was when a twenty years' service person was made redundant. We judged him to be experienced and effective. He was told directly to his face that he was being put out because a young graduate was preferred—the less able being retained, in our view. The way he was told left everything to be desired. It wasn't necessary to hurt his feelings.

Justice is often notable for its absence, as far as sufferers and survivors can see:

♦ There are people made redundant who shouldn't be (relative to others who were).
♦ The recompense for redundancy is grossly inadequate relative to the person's past contribution.
♦ It's unfair relative to the level of the pay-offs to top people.
♦ The redundancy represents a violation of the old contract.
♦ There are no clear procedures or criteria for deciding who is to be made redundant.
♦ There's no appeal or redress.
♦ The whole thing's handled with the interpersonal sensitivity of a rhinoceros.

♦ Even if it's handled well by professional outplacement consultants, this indicates they can't be bothered/face doing it themselves.

Such feelings of injustice are powerful. They can lead to anger, which may be expressed by word or deed. Nevertheless, these feelings and their expression, however deeply felt, actually indicate that people have not been changed in the core of their being. Their sense of justice and fairness remains. It is still part of their view of the world. They still believe that there should be, and often is, a fairness in the social exchanges between people. It is therefore not surprising that there exists a variety of organizational methods of managing perceptions of inequity.

If perceptions of inequity were the only consequence of restructuring, then organizations might justifiably feel some confidence. They might feel able to manage the transition to the present contract, albeit with careful handling of the ongoing redundancies and the feelings of those who remain.

But feelings of inequity are merely the tip of the iceberg. There is much, much more beneath the surface which no amount of management can melt away.

REFERENCES

1. Schweiger, D. M., Ivancevich, J. M. and Power, F. R. (1987) Executive actions for managing human resources before and after acquisition. *Academy of Management Executive*, 1, 127–138.
2. Noer, D. M. (1993) *Healing the Wounds: Overcoming the Trauma of Layoffs and Revitalizing Downsized Organizations*. San Francisco: Jossey-Bass.
3. James, K. (1993) The social context of organizational justice; cultural, intergroup and structural effects on justice behaviors and perceptions. In Cropanzano, R. (ed.) *Justice in the Workplace*. Hillside, NJ: Lawrence Erlbaum.
4. Manning, W. E. G. (1993) The content of the psychological contract between employees and organizations in Great Britain in the early 1990s. PhD thesis, University of London.
5. Rousseau, D. M. and Anton, R. J. (1991) Fairness and implied contract obligations in job terminations: The role of contributions, promises and performance. *Journal of Organizational Behavior*, 12, 4, 287–300.

6. Bies, R. J. (1987) The predicament of injustice: The management of moral outrage. In L. L. Cummings and B. M. Staw (eds) *Research in Organizational Behavior*, Vol. 9. Greenwich, CT: JAI Press.

7. Hackman, J. R. (1992) Group influences on individuals in organizations. In M.D. Dunnette and L.M. Hough (eds) *Handbook of Industrial and Organizational Psychology* (2nd edn) Vol. 3. Palo Alto, CA: Consulting Psychologists Press.

8. *National Management Salary Survey*, 1994. Kingston-upon-Thames: Remuneration Economics and Computer Economics.

9. Brockner, J., Konorsky, M., Cooper-Schneider, R., Folger, R., Martin, C. and Bies, R. J. (1994) Interactive effects of procedural justice and outcome negativity on victims and survivors of job loss. *Academy of Management Journal*, **37**, 2, 397–409.

10. Brockner, J., Tyler, T. R. and Cooper-Schneider, R. (1992) The effects of prior commitment to an institution on reactions to perceived unfairness: The higher they are, the harder they fall. *Administrative Science Quarterly*, **37**, 241–261.

11. Greenberg, J. (1990) Organizational justice: Yesterday, today and tomorrow. *Journal of Management*, **16**, 399–432.

12. Konovsky, M. A. and Brockner, J. (1993) Managing victim and survivor layoff reactions: A procedural justice perspective. In R. Cropanzano (ed.) *Justice in the Workplace*. Hillsdale, NJ: Lawrence Erlbaum.

13. Cropanzano, R. and Randall, M.L. (1993) Injustice and work behavior: A historical review. In R. Cropanzano (ed.) *Justice in the Workplace*. Hillsdale, NJ: Lawrence Erlbaum.

14. Smith, M. and Vickers, T. (1994) And what about the survivors? *Training and Development*, January 1994, pp. 11–13.

Chapter Eleven

POWER AND IDENTITY

FEELINGS OF POWERLESSNESS

Underpinning feelings of organizational inequity and injustice is the assumption that there are two parties who are dealing with each other. Each party is assumed to be an agent, having some say in what is exchanged for what. In our terms, each is a partner in the psychological contract. The assumption is seldom made, however, that employee and organization are equal partners. Sometimes employees have an edge, if their knowledge and skill is a rare commodity in the labour market. More often recently, organizations have held most of the cards. Feelings of inequity assume, nevertheless, that despite the imbalance of power, the parties still have obligations to each other, which they can and should decide upon and fulfil. Indeed, one of the functions of the psychological contract is to enable people to feel they have some control over what occurs[1].

What has happened over the last few years is that many managers and professionals have lost these underlying assumptions. They don't perceive merely an imbalance of power. Rather, they believe that they themselves are utterly powerless in the employment relationship, because:

♦ The old contract was unilaterally violated and abrogated[2]; they had no say.
♦ The new contract was likewise unilaterally imposed.
♦ The depressed labour market allowed them neither exit to other employment nor the courage to protest or act[3].

Again, these feelings only come alive when they are expressed by their owners. Here's a young man whose original psychological contract has been violated in order to save money in the short term:

> I am supposed to be a junior management trainee based at *****, but get seconded to other stores in the area as part of my formal training plan. Managers at these other stores just look upon me as another pair of hands, and do not give me any worthwhile training at all. Take this last week as an example—when I arrived at ***** they put me straight on till check-out to plug a staff shortage. They also had a "trading standards officer visit" scare on, so I was made to spend three full days just checking prices on display cabinets with packets and products. I have learned nothing this week, I am engaged as a management trainee but get treated as a general dogsbody.

The feeling of powerlessness comes through vividly in the following quotes; all the talk of performance-related pay and reward for contribution is weasel words when you have little or no control over your performance anyway:

> There is no scope for personal input; everything is centrally planned. I personally am prepared to stand (or fall) by what I can deliver, provided I have some input to targeting, admin levels, budget and resource management. Until that unlikely day arrives, the only planning I am doing is for my retirement. I believe I have a lot to offer, but "they" know best.

> Management are more and more being put in a "no win" situation, i.e. measured on performance when they have no control

over targets or resources. Due to the recession, companies know that management are unlikely to resign or complain; therefore, they just pile on the pressure. This is not a good practice as they lose management to illness, or demotivate them so much that they work to a minimum standard.

Managers believe that all that's happening is the unilateral imposition of a heavier and heavier workload from above.

There is too much expected from staff and managers. Our contracts are to work overtime when necessary; when overtime turns into the norm, something is wrong.

More and more demands are placed on staff and managers, and promises of additional staff to relieve workloads and enable managers to "manage" a sales team and staff rather than "be" the main component of that team, are ever more unlikely to materialize.

Unfortunately, at present to retain your existing position you must work much more than the thirty-six-and-a-half-hour week for which you are paid. With reduced resources and ever-increasing demands, we are now being asked to "live to work" rather than "work to live" as more and more of our personal time is required to complete our tasks satisfactorily.

Yet it's not that these managers are shy of responsibility—they'd welcome more. Rather, they lack any power over resources, so more responsibility actually simply means longer hours:

I would enjoy greater responsibility but there are insufficient resources available to me at present to make this possible; however, that does not mean that it won't happen anyway!

"Flexible" career rewards do not compensate for lost promotional opportunities due to flatter structures. Believe it or not, staff are not only motivated by money (not that there will be much of that on offer) but by the chance to manage others and assume greater responsibilities.

Managers give up hope that anything they do can have any effect on what's decided. For example, they were very doubtful that our research would be used to any purpose—just another PR job, they felt:

I welcome this opportunity to contribute. However, this will probably prove another one of *****'s "flavour of the month" projects, where we spend a lot of time, projects are set up, presentations are made, and costly implementation programmes set up, but then they are not fully implemented, or watered down for "political" reasons, and the net result—"nothing changes". The Board get good "feedback" but they never actually experience the changes and only hear what management "dare" to tell them.

I feel that any recommendations you give to improve career prospects/opportunities will have very minimal effect. ***** is going through the motions—a next step following on from a recent staff opinion survey—trying to improve image and show that they care about you as an individual—which they do not at present. But ... we live in hope!

IDENTITIES THREATENED: EXPERIENCED MANAGER

The consequence of loss of personal power is a threat to managers' identity, their notion of who they are. Many of them don't have a professional identification as engineer, scientist, etc. Rather, their work identity comes from their skills and knowledge about how to solve problems and get things done. They've come to understand a lot about organizations and how to operate in them; and about other people and how to operate with them. They've seen themselves as top management's executive arm—putting policy into practice at the sharp end. Given our Anglo-Saxon preference for activity and pragmatism over planning and reflection, middle managers had a culturally approved work identity.

It's been snatched from them in the present deal. They've been refused the resources to meet their objectives and, contrary to the buzz word "empowerment", many of them now have little autonomy in how they operate. The pragmatist and activist supreme now lacks the means to act out his or her identity. Instead of receiving adequate resources, they have themselves become resources to be disposed of by those at the top:

77

Over the last few years I do not feel ***** is interested in its staff, only results. We have been driven only to consider the bottom line, as though we are part of a balance sheet. Much needs to be done by the employer to become more interested in its staff, and to stop managing its business in a climate of fear; otherwise, if and when the economy improves, many good and talented staff will go.

One of the key elements in managers' identity is their *experience*: within and across functions in their organization, across organizations in their sector. Managers insist that they only learn through experience (although most management developers would like to add "and by reflecting on that experience"). They value highly breadth of experience, and past opportunities to take on challenging new assignments. Yet they now see their experience counting for nothing:

My organization wants to employ flexible and agile (young) heads at the cheapest rate. They believe that the rate of change in job knowledge beggars experience. You are considered to be slow, inflexible and expensive in your late 30s/early 40s. My organization will finish you before you reach 50. It makes a big song and dance about equal opportunities and discrimination in the workplace. However, you are more likely to survive if you are a black Jewish Lesbian with Aids than being over 45.

I believe management within this organization, as I have known it, has become a younger person's job. In view of my age I would not expect to be promoted further. In other words, my career has progressed as far as it is likely to. I have to look forward to, at best, a reasonably early retirement package—at worst, redundancy in the next two years with little likelihood of being able to obtain alternative employment.

IDENTITIES THREATENED: MIDDLE-CLASS ORGANIZATIONAL CITIZEN

Their identity as a manager with valued experience is not the only part of their work identity under threat. Managers have always been rather more likely than professionals to identify strongly with their *organization*[5]. Yet their identification with their employer is undermined by their insecurity. They used to come to see themselves over their careers as a BT person or an IBMer, and with a great deal of justification: they became increasingly similar in values and behaviour to the majority of others in that organization[6]. And they acquired more and more knowledge specifically about how to get things done in BT or IBM, which made them more valuable to their own employer but less valuable to others. Now that organizational identity, too, has been undermined:

> Unfortunately, a few years ago I would have strongly defended ***** but I now see it as just another company that has lost the caring attitude. Team spirit has gone, to be replaced by a "dog eat dog" environment as each member of staff attempts to protect their own job.

When your identity is organizational yet your membership is temporary and insecure, then that identity is threatened.

So, too, is threatened the *lifestyle* associated with the role of manager. Security of managerial employment and rewards led to mortgage, insurance, possibly private education—a general sense of permanence and investment in the future. Again, middle-class family identities are threatened; the visible signs and symbols are now at risk, and so is the fabric of the family relationship itself[7]:

> From a financial point of view at the present time my future looks very bleak indeed. I have had the threat of redundancy hanging over my head for the past few years (like everyone else) which will probably continue as part of a working environment. If I serve until 50 then I wouldn't be surprised if I am retired early on reduced pension. Whatever the outcome, my standard of living would drop dramatically and I would have to sell up and move down-market both in property and environment (my MTL is to age 60)—that is, if I can sell my home!

Finally, identity as *survivor* and therefore valued member of the organization is lost (or never achieved). Survivors of restructuring don't consider themselves separate, distinct and different from those made redundant. Rather, they identify with them powerfully[8]. "There but for the grace of God" they mutter, feeling guilty that they have survived while others in the team have gone. Again, it is their identity as a valued member of the organization which has suffered: they've done it to them, they can do it to me.

FEELINGS MATTER

Thus it is much more than feelings of inequity which organizations have to consider, important though these are. There are more profound psychological consequences: people feel powerless to do anything; they watch as some of the elements of their identity are stripped away. Inequity, powerlessness, loss of identity—these are profound effects, which in their turn have powerful consequences. People feel strongly indeed:

♦ Because they perceive inequity, managers feel angry.
♦ Yet they cannot express their anger because they are powerless.
♦ They are afraid to speak out because they cannot exit to another organization.
♦ They can't act, because they feel powerless.
♦ They lose trust, because they perceive the old contract violated.
♦ They lose commitment, because they have no influence on what's decided.
♦ They lose respect, because they see little respect shown to them and doubt the integrity of top management.
♦ They seek identities elsewhere since their work identities are threatened.
♦ They settle down to a cynical game of individual survival.

"So what?" top management might reply. "It's been tough for all of us, and our people just have to deal with their feelings and get on with things. It's performance and productivity that matter, not feelings." Such a response fails to appreciate that performance and productivity cannot be turned on and off like a tap, or leveraged by sticks and carrots. The profound psychological consequences of the loss of the old contract and the imposition of the new affect attitudes and feelings which in their turn affect how managers work. We argue in the next chapter that managers' reactions vary along a continuum of damage to the organization. Lowered productivity is merely the mildest consequence—wait until the sabotage really starts! It is ironic but unsurprising that restructuring measures aimed at improving productivity are likely to damage it. Once again, levers pulled have unsuspected effects on outcomes because people have ignored what's going on in between.

REFERENCES

1. Shore, L. M. and Tetrick, L. E. (1994) The psychological contract as an explanatory framework in the employment relationship. In C. L. Cooper and D. M. Rousseau (eds) *Trends in Organizational Behaviour*, Vol. 1. Chichester: John Wiley.
2. Robinson, S. L. and Rousseau, D. M. (1994) Violating the psychological contract: Not the exception but the norm. *Journal of Organizational Behavior*, **15**, 3, 245– 260.
3. Cropanzano, R. and Randall, M. L. (1993) Injustice and work behavior: A historical review. In R. Cropanzano (ed.) *Justice in the Workplace*. Hillsdale, NJ: Lawrence Erlbaum.
4. Manning, W. E. G. (1993) The content of the psychological contract between employees and organizations in Great Britain in the early 1990s. PhD thesis, University of London.
5. Van Maanen, J. and Barley, S. R. (1984) Occupational communities: culture and control in organizations. In B. M. Staw and L. L. Cummings (eds) *Research in Organizational Behavior*, Vol. 6. Greenwich, CT: JAI Press.
6. Chatman, J. A. (1991) Matching people and organizations: Selection and socialization in public accounting firms. *Administrative Science Quarterly*, **36**, 459–484.
7. Scase, R. and Goffee, R. (1989) *Reluctant Managers: Their Work and Lifestyles*. London: Unwin Hyman.
8. Brockner, J. (1988) The effects of work layoffs on survivors: Research, theory and practice. In B. M. Staw and L. L. Cummings (eds) *Research in Organizational Behavior*, Vol. 10. Greenwich, CT: JAI Press.

Chapter Twelve

THE BUSINESS SUFFERS

ADJUSTING INEQUITY

Managers and professionals have been profoundly affected by the restructurings of the past decade. Yet those in power in organizations are unlikely to appreciate more than a fraction of what the consequences will be for their businesses. Some may perceive that those on whom they relied to support them through thick and thin may be feeling a little insecure in their jobs[1]. They may understand that middle managers have lost some of their commitment to the organization which once they had[2]. They may even dimly realize that they may have forfeited some of the trust which they had previously enjoyed[3].

The consequences of these losses are bad enough. People will quickly opt out of the relational contract, since the organization has already violated it. After all, the relational contract was based on trust that each party would fulfil its longer-term promises; and that each could go beyond the specifics and help the other when opportunity or unexpected need arose. We can listen to them as they angrily refuse to undertake the "good citizen" actions which used to be part of the relationship[4]; or to even consider making the next step the organization wants them to take. Good soldiers aren't willing to march on any further; they're digging in, as one of them puts it:

> It is felt among many of the experienced managers that long-term prospects within ***** are extremely poor—irrespective of the successes currently being achieved and past achievements attained. I and several of my colleagues see a promotional move as being a temporary situation which could result in redundancy eventually, and would prefer to remain in our current situations, with a settled family life and wealth of future employment contacts should unemployment result. We are "digging in"! ***** have not made any encouraging sounds regarding future structure and stability and have therefore promoted this apparent lack of ambition, mobility and general lack of trust which is now common place among loyal and committed long-serving staff.

We can see here the beginnings of the calculating and nitpicking concern with the terms of the deal. When you've been betrayed in a relationship, you start insisting on every jot and tittle. You adjust down what you put into your work so as to make your effort exactly commensurate with your rewards[2, 5]. Now there's no more volunteering for projects, making suggestions for improvements, helping colleagues in trouble[6]. Those are actions typical of a relational contract. Instead, it's a matter of continuous adjustment of your contribution to make absolutely certain that they're not getting anything they haven't paid for.

GETTING OUT

Yet this response is typical of those who still believe that there *is* a deal, and that they *have* some say in its terms. As we argued in the previous chapter, feelings of inequity are merely the tip of the iceberg. For many, the feeling is one of acute loss of power for oneself and abuse of power by the organization. There are three basic responses to an imbalance of power of this order: Get out, Get safe and Get even.

Get out. Get out to another organization where the grass looks greener. Or get out for good. The UK unemployment figures and the employment figures are **both** down for the year August to August 1993–4; a 286 000 reduction in the case of unemployment **and** a 28 000 one in the case of employment. As Victor Keegan remarks[7], this constitutes the case of the Incredible Shrinking Workforce.

In the case of the move to another organization, individuals are using what power they have left—their labour market power. Another organization wants them for the skills and knowledge they can contribute. Hence their present organization is losing what must be a scarce labour market resource. Of course, their present organization could be greener grass in its turn for people from other equally unhappy places. But the general movement towards smaller organizations suggests that, for the larger corporations, there will be an overall loss of those people whom they should retain. Yet many of them have cut back to the bone, confident that the bone itself won't crumble away. No wonder the recruitment consultants are working overtime!

GETTING SAFE

The second response is Get safe. Personal survival in work is the individuals' sole concern. They will do just what's necessary to avoid being picked on, while putting all their energies into securing a future. Having felt betrayed by the violation of the old deal and sickened by the abuse of power at the top, they are totally cynical about the employment "contract"[8]. They keep their heads down, avoid expressing any emotions, and look out for number one. Instead of engaging in efforts to redress inequity, if necessary by conflict, they simply comply at a minimal level—what might be termed "neglect"[9]. Putting it another way, these managers are engaging in the opposite of organizational citizenship behaviour. They are not merely not going the extra mile—they're walking the required one as slowly as they can.

Their efforts at securing their future are certainly not poured into doing a better job. Rather, they curry favour with those they think have power over their future within the organization[10]. Alternatively, or additionally, they engage in what is politely termed "networking". This is supposed to be the engine for new and innovative ideas from inside and outside the organization. In reality, it's often the opportunity for a good moan about the awfulness of the organization and an exchange of gossip about possible openings elsewhere[11].

They certainly don't feel it's worth pursuing the path of skill acquisition:

> It's not what you know, but who. No one who has worked at Head Office, Regional Office, or who has ensured that they are known by the people who make career decisions, has failed to progress. They must, of course, also toe the party line at all times to ensure that no changes are questioned or disputed, even when such events are patently flawed.

GETTING EVEN

The final response is Get even. Throwing a spanner in the works is such a time-honoured practice that it has found its way into the language. Managerial and technical "spanners" are potentially far more dangerous weapons. Yet there is no reason to suppose that they won't be used. Precisely the same psychological conditions of powerlessness and frustration leading to sheer bloodymindedness are currently prevalent in middle management as were around in the heyday of worker unrest. Of course, this sabotage will be much more subtle; but, just in case you think it's inconceivable that the deferential middle classes could act in such a proletarian way, here's a couple of examples[12].

> I think I am guilty of not acting in the best interest of the organization at all times. To counterbalance the callous pursuit of efficiency, I concede all guarantee claims to customers without question. If a customer complains, I repair or replace at our cost. If I questioned more closely, or examined receipts of purchase, I am sure many would be out of date.

> There was the case of a man who left the company in a climate of considerable animosity. I don't know the details, but the

employee felt seriously aggrieved, and I have little doubt that he was justified. I remember going to his office one day to ask him a question and he said he was leaving that afternoon and it was inappropriate to get involved with my problem. Just after lunch he cleared his desk and left. It then transpired a few days later that he had adopted some personal password to gain access to his databases and he refused to divulge it. There was his PC with valuable company data on that nobody could use. Several of his close colleagues made personal pleas to him at his home, but he refused to co-operate. Eventually his section had to start completely again, and it must have cost a considerable amount of money to reinstate the system.

So the consequences of restructuring and its associated human resource interventions are not mere temporary blips in the continued progress towards the maximum possible levels of productivity. They are not due to temporary feelings of inequity and insecurity which can soon be managed away. On the contrary, they are so profound that many organizations face disaster:

♦ They are beginning to lose their best people
♦ The remainder are often doing the minimum
♦ Much effort is put into politics, networking and personal survival
♦ Sabotage is an increasingly likely response

So Get out, Get safe and Get even are not only individual reactions against the unilateral use of power by those in charge of organizations. They are also hammer blows to productivity— the very justification for the whole project.

REFERENCES

1. Brockner, J., Grover, S., Reed, T. G. and De Witt, R. L. (1992) Layoffs, job insecurity and survivors' work effort: Evidence of an inverted-U relationship. *Academy of Management Journal*, **35**, 413–425.
2. Brockner, J., Grover, S., Reed, T. G., De Witt, R. L. and O'Malley, M. (1987) Survivors' reactions to lay-offs: We get by with a little help from our friends. *Administrative Science Quarterly*, **32**, 526–541.

3. Robinson, S. L. and Rousseau, D. M. (1994) Violating the psychological contract: Not the exception but the norm. *Journal of Organizational Behavior*, **15**, 3, 245–260.
4. Brief, A. and Motowidlo, S. J. (1986) Prosocial organizational behaviours. *Academy of Management Review*, **11**, 710–725.
5. Robinson, S. L., Kraatz, M. S. and Rousseau, D. M. (1994) Changing obligations and the psychological contract: A longitudinal study. *Academy of Management Journal*, **37**, 1, 137–152.
6. Organ, D. W. (1990) The motivational basis of organizational citizenship behaviour. In B. M. Staw and L. L. Cummings (eds) *Research in Organizational Behavior*, Vol. 12. Greenwich, CT: JAI Press.
7. Keegan, V. (1994) *The Guardian*, Monday, August 22nd.
8. Mirvis, P. H. and Hall, D. T. (1994) Psychological success and the boundaryless career. *Journal of Organizational Behavior*, **15**, 365–380.
9. Kabanoff, B. (1991) Equity, equality, power and conflict. *Academy of Management Review*, **16**, 416–441.
10. Tyson, S. and Doherty, N. (1993) *Executive Redundancy and Outplacement*. London: Kogan Page.
11. Miner, A. S. and Robinson, D. W. (1994) Organizational and population level learning as engines for career transitions. *Journal of Organizational Behavior*, **15**, 345–364.
12. Manning, W. E. G. (1993) The content of the psychological contract between employees and organizations in Great Britain in the early 1990s. PhD thesis, University of London.

Part Four

THE NEW SURVIVAL STRATEGY

Chapter Thirteen

THE MANAGEMENT OF RESTRUCTURING

BETTER PROCEDURES

In response to the cry, "What can be done?", we argue that:

1. Restructuring can be so managed as to decrease the feelings of inequity often experienced by those made redundant and by the survivors. This chapter describes such management techniques.
2. However, the process of downsizing is only one of the several changes which have been forced upon managers. Others, such as increased workload, have also contributed to their dissatisfaction.
3. Moreover, many redundancies have already happened and have not been managed well. Top management's current preoccupation is with motivating those who survive after badly managed redundancies.
4. Finally, as we have argued throughout, feelings of inequity are but the tip of the iceberg. Whilst inequity may be assuaged by

careful management of the redundancy process, deeper feelings may not be massaged away so easily.

Given all these caveats, what is recommended practice for managing redundancies? It follows entirely logically from what we know about how people react to them[1]. We know that procedural justice is of the utmost importance, especially when the outcomes are really bad[2]. Procedural justice refers both to the manner in which people are dealt with and the procedures used in carrying through the restructuring. The first was ignored when yuppies in a financial institution were handed black plastic bin-liners on their way into the building and told to clear their desks! Both forms of procedural justice were absent in the following less apocryphal example[3].

> Because ***** are 14 millions in the red, all managers of my grade and above have to reapply for our own jobs. An inept way to obtain a restructuring that is degrading and demoralizing to staff. You are interviewed and then get a letter to say if you are being taken on again. I have been reappointed, but was so enraged that I helped form a delegation from the trade union. As a result these interviews have been stopped. This puny attempt to weed out the inefficient is a way that allows senior management to escape having to make choices to solve the problems of their own mistakes. They do not have the guts to call a person in and tell them straight that they have made them redundant.

It's not too hard to do better than this! The process recommendations are:

♦ The bad news should be given privately, with respect for dignity, and acknowledging both the individual's contribution and their right to feel shocked, angry, distraught, outraged or whatever.
♦ Accounts should have been given in advance of why restructuring is considered necessary, and why various alternatives are not feasible.
♦ The process for choosing who is to be redundant should be described. So should the criteria used in the decision. They should be applied with complete and visible impartiality.
♦ These criteria should be justified by argument; criteria which pay some attention to individuals' contribution and need may help balance criteria which are solely based on the organizational need.

♦ The opportunity to present a case for their retention should be permitted to individuals.

♦ The opportunity to choose from among alternative ways of exiting can increase involvement in the process and satisfaction with its consequences.

♦ The opportunity may be given to choose alternatives to redundancy (such as fewer hours, salary freeze, retraining, job redesign, job sharing, early retirement, unpaid leave, sideways moves): in sum, an inplacement strategy[4]. This is guaranteed to increase organizational commitment.

FAIRER OUTCOMES

However, attention has to be paid not only to procedural but also to distributive justice. To what extent is it possible to so recompense individuals as to enable them to feel that the extent of their loss has been recognized? And, at a deeper level, how can you give even token recognition for the contributions people have made during their employment?

Job loss can seldom be adequately compensated for. But the provision of outplacement help and generous severance payments demonstrate that the organization still cares. If part of the shock is the breaking up of a relationship, then it eases that shock if the organization continues to do more than it is minimally required to do. It implies that the organization did not terminate the relationship by choice—the bond is still there; "We're so sorry it had to end like this." Something of this comes out in the following example[4]:

> As an organization, up until about 18 months ago we had never ever made anyone redundant. When the imperative need arrived to do so, we brought in outplacement consultants to help people find new and often different careers. The trade union representative acknowledged that we did not have to do it and that the help was much appreciated. We genuinely wished to reflect the face of being a caring organization. It cost a few bob but was worth it. It helped retained staff, too; they know that if it is their turn next, or that we have to do it again, then there will be decency and help.

What's more, outplacement consultancies of repute have a good record in helping clients get a new job if that is their wish; and the severance payment can tide one over the gap. There are tangible as well as psychological and reputational benefits from equitable redundancy terms.

A CASE STUDY: BRITISH AEROSPACE

These recommendations are not pie in the HR textbook sky; they have been used and shown to be more or less effective. Perhaps the two most controversial recommendations are those about "voice"—giving employees a say in the process. Rover have given employees the "inplacement" option, and jobs were saved by *all* employees taking a cut in hours and salary. The more conventional form of "voice"—giving people choices in terms of alternative forms of exit or redeployment—was offered by British Aerospace at their Weybridge plant[5]. British Aerospace, when shutting down the plant, adopted the following strategy:

♦ Minimize collective union action by offering generous terms and moving rapidly on from announcing the closure to communicating how it would be managed.
♦ Guarantee that no one need be compulsorily out of work, and that employees could choose when they wanted to finish working.
♦ Provide a menu of procedures to help employees take decisions about their future.
♦ Offer the opportunity to transfer to another British Aerospace plant.

The aim was to retain skilled, managerial and professional employees. The provision of clear information about, and justification for, the plant closure was vindicated by the 80 per cent agreement with the statement "All things considered, I feel management made the right decision to close Weybridge". Of the workforce, 34.5 per cent went to another British Aerospace site; 31.3 per cent were permanently employed elsewhere; and only 8.1 per cent were unemployed. The majority of the young professional and skilled workers were among those transferred. Thus management's aims were mostly met.

British Aerospace was not quite so successful in meeting employees' objectives, however. This is an important point, since one would find it hard to discover a more generous redundancy programme (generous to *all* employees). In response to the statement "Looking at things overall, I feel I am better off now than I was at Weybridge", 36.7 per cent agreed, 21 per cent were neutral, and 42.3 per cent disagreed. Only 55.2 per cent felt that, as promised, they had been able to choose their own leaving date. Perhaps this was an optimistic promise given the likely operational constraints. Also, top management may have underestimated the unwillingness of some employees to come to terms with the situation. Some stayed on till the last possible moment, and used the various outplacement aids which were provided less than did others.

More seriously, those who transferred to other British Aerospace sites mostly felt less satisfied than when they were at Weybridge. They felt more stress and personal pressure, a serious outcome given that these were the employees British Aerospace most wished to retain. Indeed, the survivors were also the most negative group about the closure process itself. In this instance, this may have been partly due to the lack of co-operation from the plants to which they were transferred. However, the general lesson is that attention has to be paid to those who survive. As the authors conclude[6] "The problems lie with those that management forgot about. The first group are those who were less able to look after themselves and who remained unemployed. The second are the transferees. Their problems appear to parallel those who have been left behind in major labour force reductions which stop short of total closure. For employee involvement to work, it must be properly integrated into a more coherent company-wide personnel strategy."

LEADERSHIP AND THE FUTURE

Programmes specially designed for survivors[7] try to emphasize the future. Organizations often take the opportunity to radically restructure the remaining workforce. Sometimes this is justified as business process re-engineering—if you were starting from scratch, how would you do it? Often, it is necessary because there simply aren't enough people left to do the old jobs. Either way, it can be presented as marching into a new future. This may work the first time, but cynicism will redouble if more redundancies are imposed afterwards.

An associated tactic in managing restructuring is to emphasize leadership from the top[8]. If the chief executive can present him or herself as suffering equally and sharing everyone's pain, then people *may* identify with them and see them as an ally, not as one of the all-powerful "them". Chief executives can then lead people through the restructuring and into the future.

This is a high-risk tactic! The Chief Executive firstly has to disabuse people of the idea that he or she is actually responsible for the downsizing ("we had no choice"). Then, they have to draw attention away from the fact that they are numbered among the survivors, not the redundant. Finally, they have to walk the talk with scrupulous attention to detail; they have to be seen to work harder, have a salary *and* share option freeze, change the ways *they* work, lose *their* secretary …! A high-risk tactic indeed, but not one that has never been achieved. The heroic leaders quoted in the management literature are unfortunately seldom British.

A managing director of a medium-sized UK manufacturing business reports from painful experience: "You've not just got to share their pain; you've got to level with them all the time. And any goodwill you get you lose if you don't solve the problem. After all, you're paid more than they are for that very purpose." A far cry from new cars and salary rises concealed as share options. And a universe away from British Gas, where Cedric Brown's 75 per cent increase in salary to £475 000 per year was followed weeks later by a warning to 2600 staff in the showroom division that their salaries of £13 000 per annum were unrealistically high. This is certainly leadership from the front—so far in front as to be completely out of sight. From the Board's perspective the issues are unrelated; from everyone elses', they signify a singular insensitivity.

REFERENCES

1. Brockner, J. (1988) The effects of work lay-offs on survivors: Research, theory and practice. In B. M. Staw and L. L. Cummings (eds) *Research in Organizational Behavior*, Vol. 10. Greenwich, CT: JAI Press.

2. Konovsky, M. A. and Brockner, J. (1993) Managing victim and survivor layoff reactions: A procedural justice perspective. In R. Cropanzano (ed.) *Justice in the Workplace*. Hillsdale, NJ: Lawrence Erlbaum.
3. Manning, W. E. G. (1993) The content of the psychological contract between employees and organizations in Great Britain in the early 1990s. PhD thesis, University of London.
4. Latack, J. C. (1990) Organizational restructuring and career management: From outplacement and survival to inplacement. In G. Ferris and K. Rowland (eds) *Research in Personnel and Human Resources Management*, Vol. 8. Greenwich, CT: JAI Press.
5. Guest, D. and Peccei, R. (1992) Employee involvement: Redundancy as a critical case. *Human Resource Management Journal*, **2**, 3, 34–59.
6. Ibid., p. 55.
7. Hard, K. and Taffinder, P. (1991) Slimming is never fun. *Human Resources*, **4**, 49–54.
8. Kabanoff, B. (1991) Equity, equality, power and conflict. *Academy of Management Review*, **16**, 416–441.

Chapter Fourteen

DIFFERENT NEEDS, DIFFERENT DEALS

CONTRACTS RESTORE DIGNITY

Neither management nor leadership in the restructuring process are sufficient in themselves to enable organizations to survive into the twenty-first century. There are two basic reasons they will not suffice. First, the effects of restructuring and associated systems on many managers and professionals go way beyond perceptions of inequity; they cannot be reversed by managing the process in a fairer way. Hence, their destructive consequences for motivation, effort and productivity will continue to damage organizational performance and threaten organizational survival. Second, cost-competitiveness on its own will be no guarantee of survival. Rather, both efficiency *and* innovation together will be required for competitive advantage. The key strategic task will be to secure survival by maintaining the productivity achievements of the last decade and simultaneously developing new products or services and bringing them quicker to market.

First, the people issue. For many managers and professionals the effects have gone way beyond inequity. Indeed, one would almost welcome expressions of feelings of inequity. For such expressions would show that people still think of themselves as contracting; they still construe themselves as having agency, as being able to affect what happens to them. It is the powerlessness, the loss of identity and dignity which are the real cause for concern. As we saw, these conditions breed cynicism, excessive individualism, neglect and even sabotage. To restore power, identity and dignity would pave the way to replacing these outcomes with outcomes more beneficial to organizations and to individuals. Such restoration would constitute true empowerment.

The way to achieve it is hardly exciting. On the contrary, it sounds initially like turning the clock back and trying to reinstate an irrecoverable past. It is to engage in *explicit contracting*[1]. Contracting gives people dignity. It implies that each party to the contract, organization and individual, *possesses* something which they think the other needs[2]. Thus, contracts imply mutual *interdependence*. They imply assessment and *matching*: does what the other has to offer match my need? They imply *bargaining*: given that you can offer what I need, and I can offer what you need, what's a fair balance between your offer and mine? Given such a balance has been struck, there is then a *promissory* element: I'll guarantee to give you what I have to offer; and you guarantee me your offer in return. Finally, *reciprocity* is involved— you fulfil your side of the deal and I'll fulfil mine.

Owning, interdepending, matching, bargaining, promising, reciprocating—these are all social actions which give agency and dignity. An employment relationship which was based on explicit contracting would go far to restore self-confidence and identity. Confidence and trust in the organization would follow if, and only if, they were earned—if, in other words, negotiations are in good faith, bargains are fair and promises are kept. And the reverse is true—individuals may be held responsible to keep their side, too.

OBJECTIONS OVERRULED

The immediate objection, of course, is that psychological contracting has been demonstrated to be unworkable. The overwhelming competitive pressures of the 1980s forced organizations to break the old contract; they had no option if they were going to survive. Promises simply could not be kept. But the point about the old contract and the present one is that they were, respectively, *unilaterally* broken and *unilaterally* imposed. This need not have been the case. Explicit renegotiation could have been undertaken in the light of the changing circumstances, and therefore the changing needs, of organizations. Equally, what individuals need and what they have to offer is also likely to change over time, as they grow older or their circumstances change. Here again, renegotiation is in order. It's necessary and appropriate precisely because the needs and offers of one or both of the parties have changed since the previous contract was agreed.

Thus the psychological contract is not to be construed as a one-off agreement made when individuals join organizations. Rather, it's a periodically renewable and renegotiable bargain. Indeed, we could define individuals' careers within organizations as a series of re-negotiations of the psychological contract[3].

A second objection is to the *explicit* nature of the contract. This explicitness means that the contract has to be a transactional one, with the offers made by each party specified. The contract can't be relational, since by definition relational contracts go beyond their set terms. Yet few would be willing to return to the relational contract when it has recently been shown to be so easily jettisoned; to do so would be to invest an intolerably risky amount of oneself to a potentially fickle partner. Moreover, when the organization holds the power, the relationship can become a very paternalistic and patronizing one; we are expected to feel grateful for their generosity; *noblesse oblige*. Explicit and recorded contracts imply a business relationship between people dealing with each other on an equal footing. They do not imply ownership of one as a human resource by the other.

Contracts can't work when there is *unequal power*, it's objected. When it's not in the interests of the powerful party to keep to the contract, they can break it with impunity. Organizations have repeatedly done so in the last decade; and if skills shortages occur as projected[4], so will some individuals in the next. Yet we have argued throughout that psychological contracts can never be unilaterally broken with impunity. On the contrary, in the long run the punitive outcomes in terms of lower productivity and stifled innovation will far outweigh the temporary benefits of violation. Since long-term outcomes seldom weigh more heavily than short-term ones, however, other restraints on unilateral power are necessary.

Finally, we are asked, *where's the joy*? How can people feel they belong in an organization when they have a cool calculative relationship with it?[5]. Where's the sense of identification with the company, of affiliation and membership? But social relations and social identity at work are coming more and more from the team(s) in which we operate. It is for our immediate colleagues that we are prepared to go the extra mile, not "the organization". It is they, if anyone, whom we trust and respect. It is they who suffer the same insecurity and powerlessness as ourselves.

BUSINESS SURVIVAL AND CONTRACT VARIETY

The implications of the individual negotiating with the organization are profound. First, if individuals negotiate on the basis of their own changing needs and offers, contracts are going to differ. The apparently universal current contract of long hours and flexibility for lots of money and the privilege of having a job cannot continue to exist. Current practice implies that the only differences between people that are of importance to organizations are those of competence and performance. Yet people differ also in terms of their career aspirations and preferences. It is in organizations' interests to take note of these differences when agreeing the psychological contracts into which they enter. For their business success, we will argue, actually depends upon the co-existence of three different forms of psychological contract in the same organization.

The dilemma of typical machine bureaucracies has always been that they became less innovative as they became more efficient. Systems which successfully control processes and people render them less able to be creative[6]. The move beyond cost-competitiveness to efficiency *and* innovation is immensely difficult. Yet it is essential for survival. The UK will never be able to compete globally on the basis of cost competition alone. New Tiger economies will continue to spring up; or multinationals will site their production facilities in countries with yet lower labour costs than the UK. It is therefore imperative to retain cost-competitiveness while simultaneously fostering innovation.

Yet these two objectives rest, apparently, on two entirely different sets of values and systems. Productivity and efficiency rest upon control. They require full-time careers based on specialized expertise, while part-timers are taken on as and when required. Efficient organizations need flexibility of work; innovative ones, on the other hand, need flexibility of workers[7]. Instead of efficient but narrow experts, they need people prepared to learn new things and broaden their skills and knowledge[8].

These apparently incompatible requirements can only be met if organizations are prepared to engage in three different forms of psychological contract[9]:

1. Part-time contracts: with hours flexible to meet demand peaks.
2. Project contracts: with outcomes and completion date specified but methods less prescribed.
3. Core contracts: with learning flexible to meet organizational change requirements but some security and employability.

Part-time and project contracts help to achieve the *cost-competitive* requirement. Flexible working hours allow the most productive use of resources. Contracting out specific functions or projects secures reductions in employment costs, in theory if not always in practice. The core contract requires the other sort of flexibility—willingness to learn new skills to meet new needs. In exchange, flexible core workers retain their employability. This third contract supplies the other strategic requirement—*innovation*.

INDIVIDUAL DIFFERENCES AND CONTRACT VARIETY

So by adopting three very different sorts of contract, organizations can address the dilemma of how to combine efficiency and innovation. Yet the essence of contracting is that people want and need the different sorts of benefit each type of contract can offer. Are there differences in employees' needs that attract them to different contracts? Certainly, it is abundantly clear who prefers *part-time contracts*: unskilled and semi-skilled female workers who need the money yet need also to fulfil family responsibilities[4]. This group is augmented by a growing number of older workers who need the money and are often even more flexible as to hours than the younger female workers. Finally, there is a small but growing group of part-time managers[10]. Motives for this type of contract are financial and the desire to integrate work with lifestyle. We will rename this sort of contract "*lifestyle contracts*" in order to emphasize employees' needs.

A second set of needs are likely to motivate *project contract workers*. They are very likely to have certain other "career anchors"[11]. For example, they very often have a technical/functional career anchor. That is, they get their work identity from exercising a particular expertise. This is the one feature of their working life which they wouldn't give up—their "anchor". Project contracts appeal to them because they can exercise their expertise and develop it without having to be responsible for managing large numbers of people or to engage in organizational politics. Project contract workers may, alternatively, be heavily into autonomy and independence, another basic career anchor. The prime concern here is to free oneself from organizational rules and restrictions and have control of how, when and where one works. Project contract workers, like part-timers, are often concerned to integrate work successfully with the rest of their life. We term this sort of contract the "*autonomy contract*", since the prime need is likely to be the desire to be free of organizational shackles.

As for the *core contractors*, these employees often have a managerial anchor. They like being fully accountable for results, and are perfectly willing to become generalists. Some, alternatively, may love pure challenge. The process of winning is central for them—winning out over people or problems. These are the young Turks who are keen for promotion, power and responsibility. Or they are flexible careerists, easily bored, who welcome variety and new challenges. Core contracting will obviously also appeal to those with a security anchor high amongst their preferences. It won't be the security of the lifetime contract they will be offered, but they will still seek the security of knowing that their skills are ones which are core to the organization moving forward. Whatever the career anchor, the key for all of them will be development for the future. For this reason we consider core workers to have a *"development contract"*.

Once it's recognized that different individuals have different wants and needs, that money isn't everything to everyone, then psychological contracting can start. That is, **different** sorts of employee wants can be matched to **different** types of organizational offers. The fact that organizations are making a variety of types of offer results from their recognition of their different strategic needs—cost-competitiveness **and** innovation. How organizational wants and offers can be matched with individuals' offers and wants, and how each party's offers can be equitably bargained, we will discuss in the next chapter. The issue is: how can three very different types of contract be entered into and successfully maintained and managed?

REFERENCES

1. Handy, C. (1990) *The Age of Unreason*. London: Business Books.
2. Herriot, P. and Pemberton, C. (1995) Contracting careers. *Human Relations* (in press).
3. Herriot, P. (1992) *The Career Management Challenge*. London: Sage.
4. Industrial Relations Research Unit, University of Warwick (1993). *Patterns of Employment*.
5. Handy, C. (1994) *The Empty Raincoat*. London: Hutchinson.
6. Abernethy, W. J., Clark, K. and Kantrow, A. M. (1982) The new industrial competition. *Harvard Business Review*, **82**, 5, 69–77.
7. Eatwell, J. (1994) *The Observer*, Sunday August 7th.
8. Schuler, R. S. and Jackson, S. E. (1987) Linking competitive strategies with human resource management. *Academy of Management Executive*, **1**, 207–220.
9. Handy, C. (1985) *The Future of Work. Oxford*: Basil Blackwell.
10. Boyer, I. (1993) *Flexible Working for Managers*. London: Chartered Institute of Management Accountants.
11. Schein, E. (1985) *Career Anchors: Discovering Your Real Values*. San Diego, CA: University Associates, Inc.

Chapter Fifteen

DIFFERENT DEALS, DIFFERENT DIFFICULTIES

LIFESTYLE OR EXPLOITATION

There is far too much of the fairy-tale about our previous chapter. The happy-ever-after ending where organization and individual walk off hand-in-hand into the golden sunset is much too good to be true. Each of the three types of contract—Lifestyle, Autonomy and Development—met either the organization's need to be cost-competitive or its future requirement for innovation. By happy chance, each of them also met individuals' needs as well. Thus, each represents a coincidence of interests, where what the one party needs the other offers (and vice versa). Now we need to come down to the real world and explore some of the obstacles. Then we will be able to manage these contracts so that they stand a better chance of fulfilment.

First, the *lifestyle contract*. The happy coincidence here is between some people's desire to work part-time to allow for other activities; and organizations' requirement for a flexible labour supply to meet fluctuations in demand. Among the former are:

◆ Women (usually) who want to spend more time on family tasks than full-time employment allows.
◆ Early retirees who want to keep active and earn a bit extra, but also seek some leisure time.

In fact, these two groups are not as different in their motivation as they sound. Of a sample of UK managers and professionals approaching retirement, 48 per cent put family and personal relationships as the most important life feature for them at this stage of their lives[1].

A wide variety of forms of lifestyle contract are now available. They range from part-time work in supermarkets for women who cope with the extra demand at peak shopping hours (Friday evenings and Saturdays), to schemes of executive leasing (now retitled "interim management"). In the latter, an experienced executive can be allocated to a particular client company for as long as nine months[2]. They work as active managers, getting their hands dirty and reporting, typically, to the Chief Executive. The contracts may have long gaps between them, but while in post the interim manager has little time for the golfing, travelling, painting and sailing he or she anticipated for their 50s and 60s. Some of them have no time at all for these things—they find themselves working full-time and continuously.

The classic arrangement, however, was established by IBM in 1990[1]. Known as Skillbase, it offered 90 days guaranteed work per year to those aged 53+ who opted for early retirement. This work was initially carried out in the department from which they retired, but Skillbase has expanded rapidly. In 1994 only 25 per cent of Skillbase members are ex-IBMers, and Skillbase employees now have assignments in a wide variety of organizations internationally. A major benefit to organizations is that they have the undivided attention of an experienced individual upon one project, rather than the perils of the distractions assailing the in-house executive. Another advantage of key importance is that costs are cut, since the core full-time employees can be reduced to the bone in the sure knowledge that there is expertise available for a crisis. Similar schemes are being run by Ford UK (XR Associates); a consulting organization, Future Perfect, is available to assist in the development of similar schemes.

The major threat to the lifestyle contract, however, is the danger of *exploitation*. Organizations typically hold the whiphand, and may abuse their power. At the lower-paid levels of employment, this abuse may be evidenced by the requirement to be always on-call, even at times when the very reasons for going part-time render attendance at work impossible. In the recent phenomenon of the "zero-hour contract", firms offer no guarantee of work, pay no social overheads, offer no entitlements, but expect the "employees" to work whenever they are needed.

At the managerial level, there are indications[3] that the career prospects of part-timers suffer in comparison with their full-time peers. Perhaps this is one reason the managers in our research gave the following responses to these questions:

1. If you were offered early retirement tomorrow, how likely is it that you would accept?
    Very unlikely   –   573
    Unlikely   –   502
    Possible   –   256
    Likely   –   157
    Very likely   –   154
2. If you were offered a part-time contract tomorrow, how likely is it that you would accept?
    Very unlikely   –   813
    Unlikely   –   493
    Possible   –   219
    Likely   –   86
    Very likely   –   32
3. If you were offered help to become self-employed tomorrow, how likely is it that you would accept?
    Very unlikely   –   777
    Unlikely   –   462
    Possible   –   253
    Likely   –   100
    Very likely   –   52

To avoid exploitation, part-timers need to organize and be represented. In the case of Skillbase, this is achieved by its company status—it is Skillbase Ltd. However, we may ask what would happen if the directors of Skillbase started making unreasonable demands on *their* members! (not that there is any evidence that they have). When we leave the managerial ranks and consider operative part-timers, opportunities for exploitation are dangerously obvious. In the UK, there is little protection and few rights for these workers.

AUTONOMY OR INTERFERENCE

If the major threat to part-timers is exploitation, that to contract workers is interference. Just as exploitation threatened the basic appeal of the lifestyle contract, so interference is likely to undermine autonomy.

Underlying both the exploitation and the interference is the driving organizational imperative: cost control. Costs can be pared down if part-timers are paid as little as possible and are used only when there is a surge in demand for labour. They can also be cut if the upper rate specified to contractors is so low as to constrain the possible alternative ways of completing the job. A similar constraint occurs when the specification for the job to be done is so tight that there is little leeway for the contractors to exercise their judgement. Very often, the middle manager who is managing the contract on the organization's side has bottom-line budget targets which force him or her to exercise tight control over the contractors. Yet such control is actively hostile to the professional autonomy in search of which contractors set up on their own in the first place.

There is another source of control which threatens the autonomy contract. In an era of ever-increasing interfirm competition, organizations are likely to reveal as little as possible to their contractors of the knowledge upon which their competitive advantage depends[4]. They know that contractors are likely simultaneously or in short succession to be working for their competitors. Whatever their professional ethical stance, contractors cannot fail to use the knowledge they have acquired in previous and present jobs to assist them in their future ones. Hence both contextual and technical information which the contractor needs to do a professionally satisfying job may be withheld. It is evident that organizations have good grounds for fearing the loss of their competitive advantage. Industrial espionage has never been more prevalent.

The overall outcome is a marked reduction in the contractors' autonomy to exercise their professional judgement about *how* the job should be done. Since their work identity now rests upon their professional expertise and reputation rather than upon their organizational membership, contractors value this autonomy. After all, it's only journeymen who do routine jobs to order! Further, since they frequently left organizations in order to escape from smothering bureaucratic control, the reimposition of such control when they thought they had at last escaped must be incredibly frustrating.

DEVELOPMENT OR INSECURITY

Finally, what of the development contract? What threatens the deal whereby the core employees agree to learn continuously in order to meet creatively the ever-changing needs of the organization, and in exchange are offered the security of maintained or enhanced internal or external employability? To use Robert Waterman's phrase[5], what is likely to prevent the development of a career-resilient core?

The threat here is really a strategic dilemma[6]. It is this. How do we provide the level of security which people need in order to feel free to take innovative risks and, at the same time, introduce new people with new ideas to add the grit that creates the pearl? Given the "heads below the parapet" reaction to recent events, a degree of security is vital at the present juncture. Yet unless there is also a degree of diversity introduced at regular intervals, the core becomes a club and radical innovation is stifled[7].

Of course, if the development contract is perfectly fulfilled, then individuals derive their security from their employability. But organizations cannot guarantee internal employability; the need for regular new blood indicates that job security cannot return to its level in the old contract. And if external employability is to be enhanced, then the core employees need to think very carefully about what it is that they are learning. The inevitable consequence of rapid organizational change is that core employees will need to become more versatile. They will acquire cross-functional skills and knowledge and, especially, how to change and adapt the way their organization works. Yet this very versatility may make some of them less employable outside.

If their new knowledge and skills are transferable across organizations, or better still across sectors, then all well and good. But much of it may be organization-specific. And, as soon as they agreed to be versatile, they lost their cutting edge in their professional specialization. Technical obsolescence is now so rapid that it's well nigh impossible to get back onto the specialist track once you've forsaken it. Yet it is specialist knowledge that is a more likely guarantee of external employability, provided it's up-to-date and in demand. Movement to a smaller firm or to an autonomous contract is more feasible if you have a specific saleable skill. It is the general managers who have worked for one or two organizations only who are finding new jobs hardest to find.

So the picture is not so rosy as our previous chapter suggested. Yes, *in principle* organizational needs to combine cost-competitiveness and innovation can be reconciled with individuals' needs for a variety of outcomes. Yes, *in principle* needs for lifestyle flexibility, professional and personal autonomy and development can be met by the three different types of contract for part-time, contract and core employees respectively. Yet *in practice* there are some key threats to each of the contracts:

♦ The lifestyle contract is too easily exploited by the organization.
♦ The autonomy contract is threatened by a continued organizational urge to control and specify method as well as outcome.
♦ The development contract is bedevilled by a lack of security. This potentially inhibits organizational innovation and individual employability. If you are going even now to commit life and soul to your employer, then yet another breaking of the contract would be too awful to contemplate.

Underlying these threats to the three types of contract are problems with institutional relationships. We need to ask why organizations are so obsessed with cutting costs that they often undermine the very contracts which are aimed at achieving cost-competitiveness—those with part-timers and contractors. And we also have to try to understand why it is hard to provide the degree of security necessary to take risks, innovate and benefit from innovation. What needs to happen before we can all start with new psychological contracts which will hold?

REFERENCES

1. Curnow, B. and McLean Fox, J. (1994) *Third Age Careers*. London: Gower Press.
2. Jennings, C. (1994) Temps at the top. *Intercity Magazine*, April.
3. Boyer, I. (1993) *Flexible Working for Managers*. London: CIMA.
4. DeFillippi, R. J. and Arthur, M. B. (1994). The boundaryless career: a competency-based perspective. *Journal of Organizational Behavior*, **15**, 307–324.
5. Waterman, R. H., Waterman, J. A. and Collard, B. A. (1994). Toward a career-resilient workforce. *Harvard Business Review*, **72**, 4, 87–95.
6. Miner, A. S. and Robinson, D. F. (1994) Organizational and population level learning as engines for career transitions. *Journal of Organizational Behavior*, **15**, 345–364.
7. Herriot, P. and Pemberton, C. (1995) *Competitive Advantage through Diversity: Organizational Learning from Difference*. London: Sage.

Chapter Sixteen

INSTITUTIONS AND NEW CONTRACTS

ORGANIZATIONAL CAREER VALUES

It is tempting at this point to write an incitement to revolution. We could be asking whether the major institutions of the UK—government, city, business, media, education, etc.—are even capable of supporting the idea of contract. We might ask such questions as: Why is the financial system seen as a marketplace where savers shop around for the highest return rather than as an opportunity to invest in our nation's long-term development?[1] We might even turn all philosophical, and reflect that in most historic cultures one of the first developments towards a civilized society has been the control of the use of arbitrary power; "an eye for an eye" was not an exhortation to engage in mindless retribution but an effort to ensure that the punishment fitted the crime; it was a striving for equity.

What we will do instead is to try to specify what organizations need to look like if they are to be a supportive context for new psychological contracts. We will conduct this analysis at the level of institutions; what will be the roles of unions, the personnel function and the Board in the establishment and maintenance of the contracts? In subsequent chapters, we will be suggesting in more detail what organizations and individuals can do.

A powerful predictor of managers' career attitudes in our research was which of the eight participating finance sector organizations they belonged to[2]. How old they were and how mobile they were between jobs were also important factors. But the most powerful predictor was organization. We decided to ask the human resource specialists in each of them what it was that their organization might be doing which could result in these differences. Why was it that in some organizations managers were far more bored or far less ambitious than in others? After all, the organizations were all in the same sector and facing the same sorts of business issues.

We discovered that all the organizations were using the same HR systems (and also that none of them were using certain other systems). Both their commissions and their omissions were similar. All of them, for example, had fast-track schemes and a strong internal labour market. None of them passed on open information on likely future manpower requirements, or had developed clear policies on access to development.

So we couldn't attribute the managers' differences in attitudes to the different career management systems in use—there were few such differences. Rather, we found more subtle differences which did differentiate. These were essentially differences in values and assumptions—differences in *culture*, in fact. They reflect the basic dichotomy in values which we have emphasized throughout: are employees seen as human resources to be used as human capital for business ends? Or are they seen as individual actors who are partners in a contract? To be specific:

♦ In some organizations, employees were in the habit of nominating themselves for vacancies or opportunities.
♦ There were marked differences between organizations in access to development opportunities: an elite, or a much broader constituency.
♦ Information about career development seemed much more available in some organizations.

♦ Equity of career decision-making was more evident in some than in others.
♦ Differential account was taken of individuals' own interests in decisions regarding development plans.

EMPOWERMENT: RHETORIC AND REALITY

So the real differences at the organizational level of analysis are about values and assumptions which evidence themselves in actual behaviour[3]. This is where it is so important to distinguish the rhetoric from the reality. Consider, for example, the rhetoric of "empowerment"[4]. Over the last decade, this rhetoric has been used to express a high value placed on the devolution of decisions down the line. Yet seldom has the reality matched the rhetoric; seldom has the espoused value been evidenced in behaviour.

When we get behind the rhetoric, we see that exactly the opposite has often happened. Instead of middle managers having more autonomy, they are, in fact, more tightly constrained by ever more demanding budget targets. Top management is certainly more willing to "cascade" downwards. But what they are passing down the line are some of the pressures that they themselves are under from investors. They are delegating little real power; rather, pressure and accountability.

Another rhetorical feature of empowerment is the notion that line managers now have responsibility for the career development of their subordinates[5]. The cold-eyed response of middle managers to this idea is highlighted in our research. In answer to the question: "Do you agree or disagree with the following statement: My line manager knows no more about career possibilities than I do?" the responses were as follows:

Strongly disagree   50
Disagree   442
Neutral   332
Agree   620
Strongly agree   199

In reality, the fundamental decisions about careers are taken by top management. It is they who decide on restructuring measures and, usually, on the introduction of management fads. As far as middle managers are concerned, they are certainly not empowered to make decisions about or promises to their subordinates. They are not even likely to know very much about the current situation regarding careers in the organization—they are as uncertain as the rest. Given the probability that they won't be in post to fulfil any promises they have made, their bosses appear a broken reed for managers to rely on. All that a boss is left with is the difficult task of allocating performance-related pay.

The reality of empowerment is, in fact, in direct contradiction to the rhetoric. The major psychological boundary in most organizations is not now between management and workers. It is between top management and everyone else. Employees, including middle managers and professionals, perceive real power to be located at the top, and they are deeply suspicious about how it is used. Here is an illuminating and not untypical attribution of motive from a middle manager in a recently privatized utility:

> The organization is to be restructured in a way that appears to reflect the self-interest of existing senior management. The directors appear to have no long-term strategy for the company or its staff, and self-interest reigns supreme.

There are, of course, other possible explanations for perceived abuses of power. One is the increased isolation of top managers from the rest of the organization. It is perfectly equitable to be awarded huge pay rises and golden handshakes if the comparison is with other directors only. As President Kennedy found at the time of the Bay of Pigs fiasco, an isolated coterie fails to take account of other perspectives than its own. Chairmen still seem genuinely surprised at the outraged reactions to the recommendations of their remuneration committees[6].

THE INDIVIDUAL AND THE COLLECTIVE

Clearly, the change in organizations if a new process of contracting is going to have a chance of success is a profound one. It is likely to start with top management, and it involves new assumptions, values and behaviour. But there are other institutions involved, too: among them the unions and the personnel profession. And these institutions, too, have their rhetoric.

The unions' rhetoric contrasts the individual and the collective. The idea of the contract being an individual one is seen by some union leaders as yet another ploy by top management to divide and rule. In particular, it is seen as a principal weapon in management's efforts to weaken the unions. As so often with rhetoric, the either/or dichotomy conceals the possibility of a both/and solution. There is absolutely no reason why organization-wide agreements should not co-exist within an individual's career contract with elements tailored to their own specific wants[7].

In particular, general agreements about *how* career decisions are arrived at can be common across the organization, while the *what* of the deal, its content, can be a matter of individual negotiation. Historically, unions have concentrated on achieving content deals, primarily regarding wages, for their membership as a whole. Individual differences in wants and needs do not necessarily imply a selfish individualism, however. It is perfectly possible to act collectively in support of a process which respects individuality. If they can grasp this nettle, unions can play a major role in the contracting process.

Unions still have a solid base to build on, despite loss of members over the last decade. Support is based on the public perception that the primary reason for joining a union is protection (just what managers and professionals currently want!). In the 1989 Social Attitudes Survey, 93 per cent of respondents cited "to protect me if problems come up" as the primary reason for joining a union. Problems have certainly come up for middle managers recently, yet few of them had the advantage of unions to protect them. If they had, they might have suffered less redundancies. The third Workplace Industrial Relations Survey[8] showed that in 1990 compulsory redundancies were reported in 46 per cent of organizations without recognized unions where workforce reductions were being made, but only in 17 per cent where unions were recognized.

While unions can help with problems, their main tasks in setting up the new psychological contracts could be:

♦ To establish *general* agreements regarding career management processes.
♦ To represent individuals when top management seeks to impose new terms or to break agreed ones.

Middle managers now need little persuasion that their own interests are not identical with those of top management. Where they will need persuasion is in the area of representation. The task for unions is to present themselves as keen to represent the interests of "management"; and, in particular, whether they are willing to offer help in negotiating individualized contracts. Single-table bargaining is becoming much more frequent, however[9], so agreements regarding career management processes which are specific to middle managers and professionals are unlikely. Rather, they may enjoy the benefits of company-wide agreements, such as that at Rover, for example[10]. Their "New Deal" guaranteed no compulsory redundancies. If unions fail to seize this new opportunity, there are career management consultancies who will be delighted to represent individual clients or mediate between their clients and top management.

As for the personnel function, its aim for a long time has been to secure its survival by becoming more indispensable to top management[11]. This it has sought to do by embracing the Human Resources rhetoric and claiming the right to sit at top table. It needs and wants an input to business decisions; here is its chance. Its new opportunity is to represent top management in negotiating and maintaining the contract. The old administrative and welfare hats which personnel people have been so anxious to discard can be thrown away for good. Now, business plans and individuals' career objectives can be bargained.

Yet by adopting the HR rhetoric, the personnel profession may have made things harder for itself. In their urgent need to be seen to support the business, personnel practitioners may have thrown the mediating baby out with the welfare bathwater. They may have become so identified with top management's recent structural and process changes that they are no longer seen as committed to the notion of contract.

In reality, personnel professionals may not have been responsible for suggesting structural changes or management fads. Indeed, they may very well have pointed out some of the potentially less favourable outcomes. However, what's for sure is that they were put in charge of carrying most of them through. Hence they are now identified in employees' minds with the consequences.

In the light of this recent history, acting as top management's representatives in the contracting process is a feasible role. However, they face some major difficulties:

♦ How can they be sure that top management has abandoned its fondness for lever-pulling in favour of the contracting mode?
♦ How can they persuade middle managers and professionals that they themselves are in contracting rather than lever-pulling mode?
♦ How can they justify the more secure, developmental contracts that they will have to make with core employees to top management?
♦ How can they secure negotiating authority for themselves, rather than risk having the deals they have made countermanded from on high?

Personnel people have been identified with welfare, industrial relations, administration, systems, restructuring, management fads and Human Resource rhetoric. It's asking a lot to change tack yet again and champion contracting. Yet that's the way the business pressures for simultaneous cost-competitiveness and innovation indicate they should go. If they can't adapt fast enough, armies of consultants wait in the wings; the personnel function can be contracted out like many others.

So we have avoided the politics; and we have proposed changes in organizations, unions and personnel which may not happen. However, change can start from the bottom up as well as at the institutional level. So in the following eight chapters we ask: how may organizations and individuals establish and maintain the new contract? How may each party best deal with the four basic stages of the contracting process:

♦ Obtaining and exchanging information
♦ Negotiating the deal itself
♦ Monitoring and evaluating its progress
♦ Exiting or renegotiating

REFERENCES

1. Hutton, W. (1984) *The Guardian*, March 28th.
2. Herriot, P., Pemberton, C. and Hawtin, E. (1995) The career attitudes and intentions of UK managers in the finance sector. *British Journal of Management* (in press).
3. Schein, E. H. (1985) *Leadership and Culture*. New York: Jossey-Bass.
4. Walker, S. (1992) Empowerment: where HR has to draw the line. *Human Resources*, **6**, 98–101.
5. Institute of Personnel Management (1993) *Managing People: The Changing Frontiers*. London: IPM Press.
6. Cadbury, A. (1990) *The Company Chairman*. London: Director Books.
7. Kessler, S. (1993) Is there still a future for the unions? *Personnel Management*, **25**, 7, 24–31.
8. Milward, N. (1992) *Workplace Industrial Relations in Transition*. London: Dartmouth.
9. Brewster, C. and Lloyd, J. (1994). The changing face of union negotiations. *Human Resources*, **14**, 148–156.
10. Arthur, M. (1994) Rover managers learn to take a back seat. *Personnel Management*, **26**, 10, 58–63.
11. Cooke, R. and Armstrong, M. (1990) The search for strategic HRM. *Personnel Management*, **22**, 12, 30–33.

Part Five

ORGANIZATIONAL CONTRACTING

Chapter Seventeen

GETTING THE DATA

PRACTICALITY NOT PERFECTION

The management literature is awash with case studies of model organizations, so-called benchmarks of excellence. Accounts of those successes often have two effects upon readers: they make them think that there's one best way which they should seek to emulate—"best practice"; and they make them feel infinitely depressed because they are never likely to achieve it themselves.

We want to avoid these pitfalls in the following eight chapters. What we will try to do is to look at the process of contracting from the viewpoint of each of the two parties: top management and individuals further down the hierarchy. We will present accounts of how four organizations and four individuals actually tackled the different stages of the contracting process. There are relatively few organizations which have explicitly put the employment relationship as a strategic priority, so our choice of Hewlett-Packard, The Domino Consultancy, Rover and KPMG Peat Marwick is not surprising. What our case studies aim to show is that the psychological contract is a practical possibility rather than pie in the sky. Each of the contracting stages *can* be undertaken; *how* they are best carried through in different organizations depends upon a variety of factors known best only to themselves.

INFORMATION DISCOVERY

By way of reminder, the first stage of the contracting process is for each party to discover four types of information:

- What party wants from the other
- What party can offer the other
- What the other wants from party
- What the other can offer party

The first two of these four types of information are often treated as given. *Of course* we know what we want, and *of course* we know what we've got to offer! As an employee, I'm quite clear what I want out of my employment with this organization—or am I? Have I explored what's important to me as an individual, as opposed to what everyone else around here appears to think important? Have I noticed my priorities changing as my roles in life and my identity develop? Or would I benefit from asking myself about the relative importance in my order of priorities of such career anchors as: technical/functional competence, managerial competence, autonomy, security, service, pure challenge, lifestyle or entrepreneurship[1]?

And why should I assume that I know what I've got to offer? Yes, I'm probably aware of my experience and the knowledge and skills I've acquired over the years—though even here, I may fail to see the relevance of much of what I've achieved to the future. But what about my potential? What about what I'm capable of but don't know that I'm capable of? How can I discover my own potential without the opportunity to exercise it?

The same questions apply to the organization. Top management may have failed to analyse what it needs from its employees. It may have been so busy reducing headcount and measuring performance that it has failed to look to the future. Where does it hope to get to in the next few years, and what skills and knowledge will it need to get there? Both top management and other employees will need more than know-how based on past experience. They will need up-to-date information about their changing environment. And above all, they will need to be able to know beyond—to envisage where they would like to be and how to get there[2].

Organizations also need to check that they are sure what they've got to offer. With relentless persistence, top management insists that money is what they've got to offer. Yet attitude survey after attitude survey (for which it has paid good money) indicate that different employees want different things, and at different stages of their lives. Here is a case where, if organizations really attended to what individuals wanted, they would understand that they themselves could put forward a greater variety of offerings.

INFORMATION EXCHANGE

Which brings us on to the next issue. Granted that each party knows what it wants and has to offer, how can it find out what the other wants and has to offer? After all, I can only find out whether it's worth my while to try to negotiate a contract if I know whether the other party can offer what I want. And it will help me a lot to discover whether the other wants what I've got to offer; it's just as much a waste of time starting to talk if they don't.

If information is shared, we can estimate the likely outcomes of entering a relationship. In romantic terms[3], organization and individual can get hitched (Mills & Boon); they can remain just good friends (really!); they can play the role of reluctant suitor (Venus and Adonis); or of unrequited lover (the Cyrano syndrome). We can represent outcomes as follows:

	PARTY OFFERS	DOESN'T OFFER
OTHER WANTS	Hitched	Reluctant Suitor
DOESN'T WANT	Unrequited Lover	Just good Friends

At least they know where they stand with each other. When you know that the other doesn't want what you've got to offer, or vice versa, you can extricate yourself from any further contracting without bad feelings. This is, of course, especially useful at the recruitment stage; but it applies equally well to proposed job moves within the organization, or to such choices as whether to remain a specialist or go for a general management career.

The problems that arise when information isn't exchanged, but is guessed at or assumed, are legion. Parties can get hitched on entirely false premises.

♦ We'll promise her bigger bonuses than our competitors (when what she wants is training and development, not bonuses).
♦ They'll probably give me a major client to look after if I accept this posting (but they've actually no intention of doing so).

And so on. Admittedly, many organizations can in all honesty offer very few promises that they are sure they will be able to fulfil. This only makes it yet more important for them to admit what they can't offer as well as to offer explicitly what little they can.

HEWLETT-PACKARD, UK—INFORMATION RICHES

On to Hewlett-Packard's (HP) modern UK headquarters at Bracknell, and to Jayne Coleman, Personnel Manager. Like our following example, Rover, Hewlett-Packard has bucked the trend in its sector. While many other IT companies have had poor financial results and engaged in dramatic downsizing, HP worldwide has kept a steady financial profile during the recession, with nett income of $829 million in 1989, rising to $881 million in 1992 and $1.2 billion in 1993. Similarly, the number of employees has not fallen below 89 000 or above 96 200 during this period.

Yet HP (UK) believe they have real needs to address relating to their employees. They perceive the effects of delayering and of increased workload and productivity expectations on how employees view the employment relationship, and they are eager to address those issues. It is hardly surprising that an IT company should regard information seeking and information giving as of crucial importance in this task.

In its 55-year history, Hewlett-Packard has had only three Chief Executives. Founder David Packard retired from his role as Chairman in 1992. The well-documented "HP Way", their statement of values and objectives, still forms the ideological basis for present policies. In particular, employees are considered to be stakeholders on an equal footing with customers and shareholders. Couple this with the HP Way's insistence on the openness and accessibility of managers and of information, and HP have no choice if they are to walk their talk: they have to engage in dialogue with employees.

Which they do. In common with a number of other blue-chip companies, HP conduct an annual Employee Satisfaction Survey. Because the questions are identical across the consortium, and results are pooled, HP can benchmark itself against others, and set targets accordingly. However, when employee concerns about meaningful development in the context of decreased promotion prospects, and about the balance between work and the rest of their lives, became apparent from the survey, HP (UK) moved rapidly:

♦ HP (UK)'s Chief Executive, John Golding, chose the topic as this year's (FY1995) "breakthrough issue". Each year there is one breakthrough issue only upon which extraordinary attention is focused. This is in addition to the new strategic plans and targets and also to the "business-as-usual" elements of the business. Given the current importance of other aspects of HP's strategy (for example, Europeanization), the selection of the employment relationship as the breakthrough issue sends a powerful message. That message is that employees are considered just as important stakeholders as are customers and shareholders.

♦ One of the features of HP Quality Care is the frequency of feedback sought from customers. If the effectiveness of the breakthrough issue is to be monitored as closely, then employee satisfaction will have to be monitored much more frequently than once a year. Already, in several of the HP(UK) businesses, weekly face-to-face feedback is being obtained.

♦ The feasibility of a variety of flexible contracts of employment is being explored urgently, to offer more options for work and life balance.
♦ The three-year-old programme to encourage self-development is receiving an immediate boost, in particular in terms of:

  – the follow-up of self-development plans created for themselves by employees;
  – career planning for high achievers, in which they are helped to understand the importance of visible contribution;
  – a focus on internal and external personal marketability as the outcome of self-development.

These developments are in addition to a wide variety of other information-exchange methods already used at HP, for example:

♦ An Employee Feedback system encourages submission of compliments, comments, concerns, complaints and contributions by employees, anonymously if so desired.
♦ A Framework Profile seeks to derive from the business objectives for the future a set of Key Result Areas and Indicators. From these, in turn, is derived a profile of the skills an individual will need to develop.
♦ Appraisal is based upon inputs from superiors, peers, subordinates and customers—360 degrees plus!
♦ Weekly coffee meetings (monthly in the sales division) enable senior management to communicate current business progress and issues to the rest of the organization.
♦ Information is provided on request about gradings, pay for gradings, the gradings of other jobs and one's own pay relative to one's grade band and the going market rate.

HP is certainly information-rich. Employees can discover what the organization is going to expect of them as well as what it offers them. And top management is keen not only to learn what employees are feeling, but to do something about it fast. What's also impressive is that information is shared and learned from; feedback is the core of the learning organization.

AN INFORMATION CHECK-LIST

♦ How do employees discover what's expected of them now? In the future?

♦ Whose expectations are included in such information?

♦ How are these expectations gathered, and communicated?

♦ How do employees learn about how the business is going?

♦ How can they come to understand the implications for their own career?

♦ How are opportunities for learning and development communicated?

♦ How are new HR initiatives introduced? Do employees have any say in their introduction? In evaluating their outcomes?

♦ How does top management learn what employees are wanting?

♦ Are individual differences in wants discovered? Acted upon?

♦ What does top management know about the knowledge and skills currently available among employees?

♦ What does it know about the knowledge and skills which employees have the potential to develop?

♦ Does it seek to discover the level of commitment employees are willing to give to their work and to the organization?

REFERENCES

1. Schein, E. H. (1985) *Career Anchors: Discovering Your Real Values*. San Diego: University Associates, Inc.
2. Herriot, P. and Pemberton, C. (1995) *Competitive Advantage through Diversity: Organizational Learning from Difference*. London: Sage.
3. Ornstein, S. and Isabella, L. A. (1993) Making sense of careers: A review 1989–1992. *Journal of Management*, **19**, 2, 243–267.

Chapter Eighteen

DOING THE DEAL

RECOGNIZE DIFFERENT INTERESTS

One of the fundamental assumptions about the idea of contracting is that the parties to the contract have different wants and interests. Yet the rhetoric of Human Resource Management doesn't recognize these differences. Rather, it assumes that both have (or should have) one and the same interest only—the success of the business. Consequently, whatever is done in the name of ensuring business success should by definition be acceptable to employees. After all, whatever they want they can only get if the business succeeds; if it fails, they will be out of a job.

This assumption demonstrates a marked incapacity for understanding others' perspectives. Most top managers live to work rather than work to live. They identify themselves ever more strongly with their organization's success or failure; and with good reason. For, despite the rhetoric of empowerment, it is they who are held responsible by the key stakeholders.

Yet to project one's own concerns and priorities onto the other is a terrible danger in negotiating. Skilled mediators, such as representatives of ACAS, only succeed because they understand where each of the protagonists is coming from. Yet top management always seems to be in danger of assuming that others want what they want: the success of the business, achievement, power, money and recognition. As far as top management is concerned, very few of Schein's career anchors (see p. 103) may even occur to them as being the driving force behind their employees' career motivation. Managerial competence, of course; pure challenge and entrepreneurship, perhaps; but technical competence? autonomy? security? lifestyle? These are beyond their ken in many cases. Or, worse, some of them assume that people with these career anchors are less able by definition to contribute to the business.

DON'T ABUSE POWER

So the first requirement for successful career contracting is to recognize diversity of interest, and therefore acknowledge that the bargain struck needs to meet the needs of the individual as well as those of the business. The second requirement is related. It is to recognize that current labour market power cannot be the sole determinant of the bargain struck. It could be argued that for the last four years, the psychological contract has not existed as a contract for many. If contracting involves exchange, then many have not contracted. Rather, they have been coerced into accepting whatever was offered, knowing that if they did not accept, they would be out of work. Contracting implies negotiating and acceptance, rejection, or compromise by both parties of a deal. It implies that because both parties have taken decisions, they are more likely to be committed to those decisions[1], especially when they experience the other fulfilling their side of the bargain.

There are, therefore, two good reasons for contracting rather than exercising unilateral power. The first is the greater likelihood of mutual commitment; the second is what happens when the labour market boot is transferred to the other foot. The exercise of power works both ways. When there is a seller's market, as there is now in some specialities and soon will be in many more[2], then we will be getting more holdings to ransom like this recent exchange between a City dealer and his merchant bank employer: "I made thirty million for you yesterday. I want a million of it, or I'm going elsewhere."

BE FLEXIBLE

A third organizational requirement for successful bargaining is to be flexible, both in terms of what it wants and what it offers. Few strategic plans can be specific enough to detail the precise knowledge and skills which will be required. Many organizations are reduced to recruiting or promoting on the basis of evidence that the individual is good at learning and capable of working with others. This renders detailed person specifications of doubtful value, particularly if they retain specific arbitrary requirements such as degreed status.

Organizations also need to be flexible about what they can offer. If the likely success of the negotiation is partly dependent upon them offering what the individual wants, then the value of individualized bargaining becomes evident. Organizations can fail to achieve agreement by offering what the individual has little desire for; or, they can be forced into a more expensive offer than they need to be. A little extra lifestyle perk such as more holiday could be of equal value to the individual as a large increase in salary—but it could cost the organization a whole lot less.

BE FAIR

A final requirement is to realize that the negotiating process itself has to be equitably managed. It is usually the organization that sets the scene and provides the props. It has the process power, in so far as it provides (or fails to provide) the opportunity for career discussion. If, for example, that formal opportunity occurs only in the last ten minutes of an annual performance appraisal meeting, then the dice have already been loaded against the individual. If no formal opportunities are provided, then individuals may find it hard to initiate a negotiation. If bosses are not prepared for such an approach, then their shocked response may prejudice the outcome.

Of course, where the negotiation is the initial one at recruitment, the process is usually demonstrably one-sided. In the typical selection interview, the questions are asked by the interviewer and answered by the applicant. When applicants are invited to ask questions at the end, they usually construe the invitation as a further assessment device; will I ask the right question, they wonder?

Very often, the organization is represented in the negotiation by a personnel manager or in the person of the individual's boss. Either way, the resources that this representative brings to the negotiation are greater than those of the individual. Personnel can claim that they have authority from top management and use it to justify their negotiating limits. The line manager has other power—for example, appraising the individual's performance and determining rewards.

So procedural equity needs careful attention. Assuming both parties have shared the appropriate information, do they have equal opportunity to put their case? Could the availability of a mentor or some other supporter be of use to the individual? How are deals to be agreed and recorded in some form so that they can be referred to subsequently?

For sheer flexibility and mutuality, however, we need look no further than to Domino Consultancy and its Managing Director, Geraldine Bown.

THE DOMINO EFFECT—ORGANIZATIONAL NEGOTIATION

Geraldine Bown is the founder of the Domino Consultancy, a company with a strong reputation for its work on equal opportunities issues, and the development of women in the workplace. From the commitment of one woman it grew to a staff of 14, with a projected £million turnover. In 1993 the business was badly hit by recession, the target was not achieved and Geraldine took the decision to change the basis on which the business was organized. In each stage of the organization's life, she has had a clear sense of how she wants to negotiate with those she employs. She has also experienced the downside of the contract becoming out of balance.

When the business started to grow, she allied the basis on which she employed people to the same principles she used in managing the business. Just as she saw her growth strategy as being based on always being one step ahead of the client's ideas, and therefore having to move quickly in response to emerging trends, so she saw her staff as also being developed to be one step ahead. Every new employee knew that they would be encouraged to grow in response to changing demands. A freelance writer became a company director, a PA became a sales executive. The deal worked because the greed of the business for skill was matched by the desire of individuals for development.

Since Domino did not prescribe solutions to its clients, but listened to their story, Geraldine held as a principle that no idea put forward by her staff would be automatically dismissed. When, after she had just leased a three-storey building three of her staff announced they would prefer to work from home, she listened. Having listened, she decided to give greater weight to the spin-offs in terms of employee performance over the business costs of wasted space. Having accepted their case, she then supported them by providing the technology that would enable them to work effectively from home. When challenged about the risk of giving such autonomy, her response was that the ultimate check on the effectiveness of the policy was not her, but on whether it enabled staff to meet the expectations of their clients.

The acting out of her personal principles was visible in the deals which she offered. When employing women returners, she would get them to define the hours they wanted to work, rather than regulating when people would work. She gave her staff responsibility for drawing up their own job descriptions, and allowed them to use whichever job title they felt would help them in their role. She gave staff the option of a childcare allowance or private healthcare, and gained press attention for being the first company in the UK to employ a company nanny. While such offerings seemingly made Domino a model employer, Geraldine Bown came to recognize that her principles of fairness could backfire.

In her concern to give equal treatment to all, she found herself trapped by her own beliefs. When two new consultants were taken on at the same time and offered the same starting salary, one of them accepted and one negotiated for more. Having agreed to her request, Geraldine then increased the other's salary offer on the grounds of fairness. When the same consultant asked to work from home, she agreed and offered to pay her petrol costs in travelling to the office, as this offer had already been made to an existing home-based worker. A third consultant who had relocated then claimed that as she didn't receive a petrol allowance, her removal expenses should be reimbursed. Once again, Geraldine accepted the fairness of the request. When, finally, petrol allowances were discontinued and instead incorporated into a new pay package, staff expected that the payment should cover their tax considerations on their petrol costs.

Both staff expectations and the organization's offers went beyond the monetary. While all staff were allowed two days a month study time, when a new member of staff negotiated for fees and additional time off for completing a Masters degree, Bown then felt she had to agree to a similar request the next year. A scenario of fairness from her perspective was both strangling her and raising expectations from employees of what was on offer. Ironically, it also worked against her. When the going got tough, rather than her previous generosity earning her goodwill, the removal of offers caused a loss of trust, and increased employee insecurity. Her learning from this experience is that concepts of universal fairness are unworkable because boundaries of expectation can extend beyond a point which is tenable from the organization's perspective. For the future, her contracting process will be based on individual negotiations related to individual needs, rather than universal rights.

Along with her belief in personal autonomy, she believed there was a joint responsibility for the sharing of information. Each month employees were given all the business figures apart from details of each others' salaries. They were able to see the profitability of each others' work and to ask questions of each other. A policy which grew from a belief that ownership required openness, in retrospect, also presented Geraldine with a downside. The openness was read as a right to power in decision-making. This had not been an intended part of the deal. While she had seen information as helping decision-making by consensus, but with ultimate decision-making being in her hands, it was seen by some employees as the right to direct decisions. The result was resentment when suggestions were not accepted. In retrospect, she would more clearly state the rights which access to information gives.

While sharing information is a key principle of how she believes people should work together, she also admits that when times got tougher it made the management of the process more difficult. Employees were not protected by ignorance. There was no hiding of the monthly decline in income, and people's anxieties turned into a tendency to blame. Those who delivered training blamed sales personnel, whilst sales personnel saw themselves as having to try and sell the skills of trainers which did not match market requirements. As Geraldine struggled to find a way through which matched with her principles, she admits vacillating before taking the tough decision to change the whole structure of the business.

The company now only retains on its payroll sales and support staff. Attached to the organization, however, are 20 associates; self-employed consultants who work for Domino when their skills are needed. Such a shift could have marked a philosophical change, a disillusionment with people management, and a preference for a strict client/contractor relationship. Such a deal would not match with the values Bown sees as central to Domino.

Her new recruitment process is one in which, once interested, consultants have been exposed to Domino. They are invited to write a proposal on what they could offer Domino's clients. From Bown's perspective, it means that the range of skills she now has to sell clients is potentially far greater—and they are held by people who have experience and expertise. Where previously she had nurtured growth and accepted the implications for service delivery, she now has greater quality assurance.

If individuals are offering her their expertise, Domino is offering them a package which supports them in doing their job effectively. She knows that for self-employed consultants the difficulty of balancing sales/marketing effort against income earning can be stressful. Domino offers them freedom from that demand by selling their skills into organizations, whilst giving them commission on any sales they make on Domino's behalf. If consultants use their own previously generated work whilst on assignment with Domino, the copyright for that work remains with the author. Since it is important that clients should see all consultants as representing Domino, the company gives complete administrative back-up in the design and production of materials and the handling of all practical arrangements. Even more radically, the pay rate for the consultant does not necessarily relate to the client pay rate. If a consultant requires a £500 daily rate, and the client will not agree to a fee which will deliver the desired gross margin, Bown will guarantee that daily rate to the consultant if she believes the rate is merited by the potential of the client or the skills of the individual. In this way she protects consultants from becoming embroiled in competitive mark-downs on their pay rates.

The deal is not one way. Consultants are required to sign a Domino Charter, which lays down the principles to which Domino works, but also makes it clear that if their work does not match with quality expectations the contract will be ended. The contract will also be ended if any consultant, in their own right, accepts work from a Domino client, instead of it being handled by Domino. From Geraldine Bown's perspective the new deal is working well. Instead of feeling she has to please her employees, they now have to please her as their client. Instead of being limited by a belief in the development and encouragement of individuals, which inevitably led them to want to move on once their confidence had grown, she no longer is being constantly hit by the business costs of their development. From clients' perspective, service delivery has improved, because the directors can concentrate more on customer service than employee satisfaction.

The change has not been an easy one. The letting go of staff to whom she felt strong loyalty and responsibility caused her much personal pain. However, she has also learned from the process that when negotiating as an employer, the balance between the two interests has to be maintained.

A NEGOTIATING CHECKLIST

♦ Does the organization ever engage in career negotiations (i.e. does it change its offers to accord with employees' wants and offers)? *continues*

continued

♦ Does it engage in negotiations only when there's a seller's labour market?

♦ What sorts of employee want is the organization prepared to take into consideration:

    – functional preference?
    – training and development?
    – family situation?
    – reward preference?
    – a degree of security?
    – external employability?

♦ What sorts of employee offer is the organization prepared to take into consideration:

    – existing expertise?
    – development potential?
    – development willingness?
    – functional flexibility?
    – organizational commitment?

♦ Does the organization provide explicit opportunity and occasion for career negotiation:

    – how often?
    – as a separate meeting, or as part of another?
    – at whose instigation?
    – who represents the organization?
    – can the individual ask for representation?
    – are the outcomes recorded?

REFERENCES

1. McFarlin, D. B. and Sweeney, P. D. (1992) Distributive and procedural justice as predictors of satisfaction with personal and organizational outcomes. *Academy of Management Journal*, **35**, 3, 626–637.
2. University of Warwick Industrial Relations Research Unit (1993). *Patterns of Employment*.

Chapter Nineteen

CHECKING UP

CHANGED WANTS AND OFFERS

There are all sorts of reasons why the parties need to check up periodically on whether the psychological contract is working. First of all, each of the four basic elements of information on which the contract is based may have changed over time:

1. The organization's wants will have changed. Notions of deciding on a vision of where the organization is to go, and then sticking to a plan to get there are textbook prescriptions rather than rough reality. As circumstances change, vision, too, changes. Strategy, as Henry Mintzberg[1] puts it, is "emergent". Visions become merely Utopian if their possibility of attainment shrinks to zero. Thus a long-term detailed Human Resource plan is for most organizations entirely inappropriate. Rather, the skills and knowledge they want for the future will change as their vision of that future changes. As we have argued, the present need to

add innovative capacity will result in organizations wanting people who can learn, and who can learn to learn.

2. The organization's offers will change, too. The old offers of long-term security and regular promotion have gone for ever. Currently, much less is on offer: typically, having a job at all, and relatively high monetary rewards. In the future we can expect the offers to diversify, with the core contract offering employability as a form of security.

3. Individuals' wants are also on the move. This will partly be a function of the development of the individual's life and the particular roles which are prominent at any particular stage in their life[2]. How many enthusiasts for foreign postings in their 20s are equally enthusiastic in their 30s? But it will also change as a result of a change in the cultural zeitgeist. Currently, commentators claim to detect a gradual abandonment of selfish Thatcherite individualism in favour of greater community values. There is, indeed, some evidence from the USA that career aspirations reflect general cultural movements[3]. For example, managers brought up in the counter-culture of the 1960s subsequently had less respect for authority, less need for the approval of their bosses, less religious or humanistic orientation and less heavily masculine attitudes.

4. Finally, what individuals have to offer is fluid, too. While their specific technical expertise may lose its cutting edge for a variety of reasons, interpersonal skills and wisdom and business awareness may increase over time.

CHANGED BEHAVIOUR

So a contract has to be monitored in case parties' wants and offers have changed since it was first established. But that is not the only reason. The balance of the exchange may have shifted, too. Perhaps one or the other party has unilaterally started offering less than they originally agreed; they may feel confident in doing so because their power in the labour market has increased in the interim ("Why worry—I can get a new job/a new person without much trouble now"). Alternatively, one or the other breaks the agreed procedural rules—they do things the wrong way. Organizations, for example, may start ignoring some of the checks and balances they had built into the promotion procedure to ensure equity. Or individuals may consistently by-pass their line manager in career discussions, although he or she is responsible for their career development.

A very common situation is where one party adjusts what they offer because they perceive the other to have changed what they provide. Graduate recruits may feel that they have not been given the training they were led to expect, so they reduce effort and commitment. Alternatively, they feel that, after two years, they've invested time and effort in the organization, and therefore deserve more in return[4].

As we have argued, potentially damaging responses of anger, mistrust and powerlessness may result from such perceived inequities. So it is important for any changes in what each side supplies the other, and for any consequent feelings of inequity, to be discovered and addressed. Unless the keeping of contracts is monitored and readjustment or renegotiation occurs, the alternative can be exit from the contract. While exit by one party or the other may be the appropriate outcome, it's important that this should be based on an agreed failure to renegotiate rather than on immediate feelings.

ROVER: MONITORING THE MANAGERS' DEAL

One of the few UK business success stories in manufacturing of the last few years is Rover. Announcing in 1994 new models and a recruitment drive for 1500 new jobs, they have bucked the trend famously. Yet when Graham Day arrived in 1986, they were faced with a huge battle to survive. It took a panoply of the usual measures to turn them around but, as we shall describe, it took a lot more as well.

Costs had to be cut rapidly, and radically, and downsizing and delayering occurred with a vengeance. More than 1000 white collar and managerial employees were made redundant, and eight management levels were reduced to four. At the same time, a powerful

Total Quality Management programme was introduced, with the aim of "extraordinary customer satisfaction". The influence of Rover's business partner at the time, Honda, was clearly evident in this programme. It was led by top management, who committed completely to the programme and led others by coaching and example to follow suit.

Our informant, Nigel Sullivan, Personnel Manager working at the Swindon plant, described the overall outcome of these changes as profound and broad-ranging. There were new processes and structures in place, as well as the typical change in culture consequent upon a successful TQM programme.

♦ Working *processes* now emphasized adding value and the involvement of those who had the requisite skills and knowledge ("factholder involvement").
♦ Organizational *structures* were now based on products and parts rather than on functions. Job roles were more broadly defined, and project teams were common.
♦ Organizational *culture* moved from compliance towards commitment—"a sense of shared destiny". New values of trust and empowerment were espoused.

In order to demonstrate their commitment to the workforce, top management next negotiated with the unionized workforce, some 30 000 in number, a "New Deal". In exchange for flexibility of working practices and less demarcation, together with the removal of the clocking-on and clocking-off system, top management made a dramatic pledge: there would be no further compulsory redundancies.

As they evaluated the outcomes of the "New Deal", top managers noticed very considerable disquiet among middle managers. Above all, middle management feared the loss of control over employees which they felt would ensue. Without the fear of redundancy, and without the clocking-on system, they had no stick to beat the donkey with and no fence to keep him in. What's more, while the workforce was lucky enough to be represented by unions, the same "no redundancy" pledge had not been made to them. Yet they had seen their colleagues decimated a few years earlier.

Perceiving these possibly unforeseen responses, top managers realized that they needed to redress the balance of their deal with middle management. Yes, they had removed the tools of control and compliance from the middle managers' toolkit. What could they offer in its place?

◆ *Autonomy* in how the new values were implemented. Top management showed that it trusted middle managers to put values into practice in a variety of ways. The consequence is a range of practices even within similar work units, ranging from detailed checklists to no managerial checking at all.
◆ *Support* in their new leadership roles in terms of the offer of coaching.
◆ *Self-assessment* in the form of a performance and development review, which covered personal as well as business objectives. In line with Honda practice, successes were celebrated and needs for help were identified.
◆ Their own "*New Deal*". This was not explicit, but managers came to realize that they were not being made compulsorily redundant either, and that they were getting the same benefits (such as paternity leave and added leave for long service) as the workforce enjoyed.

So top management sought to equalize the deal with middle management by offering more, to compensate for the control middle managers felt they had lost. But how was this new deal for the middle managers subsequently monitored? The response Nigel Sullivan gave us was most interesting. He said that there was no need for explicit monitoring: the deal was now so firmly embedded in the culture that it was monitored and enforced by the norms of the organization. In effect, everyone monitored the deal. From top management's point of view, they knew automatically that the deal was on course because people still kept coming to them for help, and kept getting involved and moving around. The exceptions to these norms simply got "left behind".

However, it wasn't just top management which expected that middle management would follow the norms: it was the workforce too. They naturally came to expect support from managers in the same way as they supported each other in their work teams. There were expectations up from the workforce as well as expectations down from the top. Of course, top management had encouraged the workforce to hold these expectations of the management; but the overall Rover message is that everyone monitors relationships in the workplace when there are clear norms about how those relationships work.

A MONITORING CHECKLIST

♦ Does the organization check up on whether it already has the skills and knowledge that meet its present needs? If so, how often? How does it find out?

♦ Does it check up on whether it is in the process of developing skills and knowledge to meet its likely future needs? If so, how often? How does it find out?

♦ Does it review the nature of what it offers its employees in the light of their changing wants, and of market practice?

♦ Does it monitor labour market trends so as to discover the likely availability of skills and knowledge?

♦ Does it check up on the fulfilment of the contract? From its own perspective only (is the employee fulfilling his or her side of the bargain)? Or from the other perspective as well (does the employee feel the organization is fulfilling its side of the bargain)?

♦ How does it do so? How often? Who owns the resulting information? What's done with it?

♦ Does it monitor the satisfaction of both parties with the existing contract?

♦ Who is responsible for doing all this monitoring? What resources do they need to help them?

REFERENCES

1. Quinn, J. B., Mintzberg, H. and James, R. M. (1988) *The Strategy Process: Concepts, Contexts and Cases*. Englewood Cliffs, NJ: Prentice-Hall.

2. Super, D. E. (1980) A life-span life-space approach to career development. *Journal of Vocational Behaviour*, **26**, 282–298.
3. Howard, A. and Bray, D. W. (1988) *Managerial Lives in Transition: Advancing Age and Changing Times*. New York: Guildford.
4. Robinson, S. L., Kraatz, M. S. and Rousseau, D. M. (1994) Changing obligations and the psychological contract: A longitudinal study. *Academy of Management Journal*, **37**, 1, 137–152.

Chapter Twenty

RENEGOTIATE OR EXIT

RENEGOTIATE

One of the major current sources of trouble in the employment relationship is that contracts get broken and nothing is done about it. Individuals do not dare to seek a renegotiation, and they are unable to exit. They consequently adjust down what they offer, to match what they perceive to be a reduction in what the organization is now offering. And they feel increasingly angry at the inequity they are fighting against.

Organizations, on the other hand, may see no need to renegotiate. They may be unaware of perceived inequity, or unconcerned about it. Moreover, they may have a long tradition of negotiating at particular stages in an individual's career. Entry is the most obvious point, and there are still some organizations for whom it is the only point—essentially, the negotiation involved buying into the career system at entry and surrendering yourself to its tender mercies thereafter. More organizations treat certain key transition points as occasions for renegotiation. For example, if you are an engineer or a scientist, do you broaden from your expertise at around 27 and 28, or do you negotiate a technical career? When you come to the point in middle management at which a further promotion becomes unlikely, how do you negotiate the rest of a plateaued career?

Both of these rationales for renegotiation are now outmoded. The former implies a buying-in by the individual to the organization for life; the latter a structure of age-stage career development which today applies much less. Rather, organizations need to renegotiate:

♦ Whenever wants and offers change
♦ Whenever the existing contract is in trouble

What's more, they must be prepared to renegotiate a different type of contract, to meet changing wants. In other words, the employment relationship is likely to be enhanced if the organization is prepared to move from, for example, a full-time to a part-time contract to meet an individual's changing lifestyle needs; and then to move back again to full-time if appropriate.

Given the importance of renegotiating each contract with each individual when necessary, organizations are going to have a problem with equity. When each renegotiation results in a different deal, people will compare their own existing deals with the new one they see struck with someone else. Perhaps the only way of managing perceptions of inequity is to monitor all contracts often enough to persuade individuals that their own deal is always a fair one *for them*. The more varied people's deals are, the harder it is to make comparisons since like isn't being compared with like. Unfortunately, everything that we know from research and experience tells us that comparisons, while odious, are universal. An organization may be able to accommodate individual wishes to go part-time, for example, for the first ten who request it. When it becomes a deluge it may be a different matter, but we can be sure that when number 11 is refused, he or she will feel *very* hard done by.

EXIT

Let us suppose that attempts at renegotiation have failed, and exit is the only course. How to manage exit also requires careful organizational attention. Those who leave are still potential assets.

1. Suppose the organization would have liked to retain them, having spent a great deal on their development. It can still gain credit for having benefited its business sector community, as German companies do[1].
2. If the exit follows a negotiation where both parties are agreed that exit is appropriate, then the exiting employee will perhaps become a valuable business ally in their new organization.
3. They may even subsequently return and rejoin, a sequence actively favoured by some of the large UK accountancy firms.
4. Even if the decision to exit is unilateral, by individual or organization, it can be managed so as not to damage either the organization's reputation or possible renewed relations in the future[2]. The scapegoating of those who leave or are made redundant is not uncommon; it can be highly damaging.
5. Finally, if individuals move on to good jobs, their organization will be seen to be offering good employability prospects. It will thus attract good recruits.

So overall, renegotiation of and exiting from contracts are very important for the organization. As we can see from this case study from KPMG Peat Marwick, it *can* be done.

KPMG PEAT MARWICK—TWO TYPES OF PARTNER

David Westcott is the Personnel Partner of KPMG Peat Marwick, one of the largest firms of chartered accountants in the world. In the UK there are 600 partners, and 9000 employees in total. In order of volume, the different services offered are: audit; tax; management consultancy; corporate finance; and corporate recovery.

The nature of career progression in the accountancy profession still follows a well-defined route. There is still a close relationship between age and grade, with the inevitable consequence that if you fail to make the grade by a particular age you may be permanently handicapped in the career tournament. Starting with a largely graduate entry at 21 or 22, *recruits* are given a three-year training contract. During this time, they do a lot of basic auditing work, partly in order to meet the Institute of Chartered Accountants qualification requirements. Having passed their qualifying examinations at 24/25, and gained another two or three years of experience working with clients continuously, they then become *managers*. In this role, they lead small teams and allocate resources for a variety of assignments. By 30/31, they are promoted to *senior manager*, responsible for managing several assignments simultaneously, and leading a department typically involving 30 to 40 subordinates. For the first time in their careers, they are not in a primarily hands-on role. Rather, they spend most of their time in administrative and project management roles. They are responsible for the delivery of jobs to the satisfaction of the partner who has negotiated the contract with the client. Finally, at around 34/35, they become *partners*. Partners manage the relationship with clients, and are responsible for initiating, establishing and maintaining that relationship.

There are several crucial transition points in this career sequence:

1. The period after qualifying and before manager. Many leave at this point. They always intended to obtain a useful business qualification and then move away from a professional firm altogether, into merchant banks or industry. Others decide during the qualification period that the profession is not for them, or KPMG persuade them that it isn't. Others again are seduced by attractive offers from firms who seek to take advantage of an expensive training paid for by another company.

2. The move between manager and senior manager. Here, those who enjoyed client contact have to come to terms with a more back-room, managerial role where their main clients are now their own firm's partners. What's more, moves out tend to be harder from now on, since the work of senior managers is specific to the chartered accountancy profession. The die is cast.

3. The transition to partner. Again, a fundamental change occurs in the nature of the work. Partners represent the firm to clients. They have a strong marketing role in order to initiate and establish client relationships. Moreover, once the relationship is established, they are expected to devote their lives to maintaining it. There is no part of their lives (apart, hopefully, from their annual leave) which is immune from client service. They can be called

149

upon for help at any time, and their social and business lives are inextricably interwoven. While managers and senior managers work long hours, at least they know when work is over for the evening; partners never have this luxury.

We decided to look in more depth at two of these three transitions. We asked David Westcott how KPMG managed the exit process after qualification; and how they renegotiated the contract when people entered the partnership.

First, *exit*. During the final year of the three-year qualification period, KPMG try to decide which 400 or so of the 500 who have survived thus far they wish to retain. This they do on the basis of formal appraisals and informal discussions with their line managers and responsible partners. During 1990–93, the task of retaining those they wished to retain was easy; there were few predators seeking to poach them, and the main problem was providing them with enough of the scarce work available. Now it's quite the reverse. Many of them are headhunted with offers they think they can't refuse, so KPMG's task is to persuade them in advance of qualification that there are career benefits KPMG can provide which surpass those being dangled before them by others. Discussions might include a move away from rather boring audit to tax or corporate finance, or even to sexy consultancy. A secondment overseas at what is often an attractive stage of one's life for such an adventure might also be on the cards. A secondment to a client or to a Government department are other available options. KPMG are currently considering the introduction of formalized career workshops at this juncture, rather than the present informal discussions.

While there are many whom KPMG wish to retain, there are some whom they don't. These are given advance advice that they should think about leaving the organization. No specific timescale is set at this point, and a blind eye is turned to time out spent looking for another job. KPMG call this process "counselling out". The aim is that both parties agree that it is in both their interests to part company. Westcott admits that partners and senior managers differ in their ability to achieve this agreement with their leavers. However, he maintains, "It's important that people leave feeling good about us. One day, they are our clients." Dismissal or redundancy is the last resort, and nowadays is an infrequent occurrence.

Those who leave KPMG, whether KPMG wanted to retain them or not, are treated as alumni. They usually stay on the mailing list for professional information sheets, and are invited to two or three events a year. The degree of contact with alumni tends to be based on the regard with which they were held and the nature of the firm they've gone to. KPMG don't send too many professional updates to Price Waterhouse!

Now for *renegotiation*. KPMG make a huge effort to be explicit to senior managers about what the move up to partner entails. At a development centre, senior managers are faced with exercises requiring them to market KPMG to prospective clients. Despite the coolness of the KPMG partner playing the role of the client in this simulation, the potential partner is expected to display ambassadorial skills. KPMG also hold workshops for senior managers, at which valued clients tell them what sort of service they have come to expect from KPMG. Outstanding partners then go through the type of service behaviour and level of commitment that has resulted in these satisfied clients.

KPMG has made explicit the new expectations it will be holding of senior managers if they become partners. It has also made clear the benefits which the status of partner brings in terms of ownership of the firm. Senior managers often make clear in return what they want and have to offer. Some are unwilling to take on a marketing and relationship management role. Others want to maintain and enhance their professional expertise—to become *the* expert on VAT, for example. Others, again, lack the initiative and innovation to seek new clients and services; they have had all the go knocked out of them by the grind of auditing through a period of recession and commercial scandals.

Whilst some few technical experts are made up to partners, most of these responses are considered incompatible with partnership status. Senior manager and KPMG will negotiate an alternative: a career as a respected expert senior manager, for example, or exit. KPMG often seek opportunities for exiting senior managers with their clients.

The two features of renegotiation and exit at KPMG which stick out are, first, its *explicitness*. Instead of the old "tap on the shoulder" routine, clear information is given explicitly and face-to-face (though not always formally). While the organization is explicit, however, we were not aware of any unusual methods KPMG used to encourage reciprocal openness from their staff. Westcott assured us that at their annual appraisal interview they often spontaneously requested new developmental experiences. The second aspect of note at KPMG is the treatment of those who leave as a potential *valued resource*. This is in marked contrast to the scapegoating and bad-mouthing of those departing from many organizations. But we conclude by a little naughty speculation. How long will professional firms like KPMG be able to maintain their rigid age-stage hierarchical structure and up-or-out philosophy when business and demographic trends militate against them?

AN EXIT CHECKLIST

- ◆ Does the organization know the number of those who exit voluntarily from different levels of the organization?
- ◆ Does it ask whether these are employees whom it is willing or unwilling to lose?
- ◆ Has it sought to discover whether there are particular career points at which employees are most likely to leave voluntarily?
- ◆ Does it make efforts to discover why employees leave? Are they dissatisfied with their existing contract? Would the organization have been willing to renegotiate in order to retain them?
- ◆ How big are the changes, if any, in an employee's contract which the organization is prepared to renegotiate?
- ◆ Does the organization inform those who remain of the destinations of those who leave?
- ◆ Does the organization maintain contact with those who have left? Is it willing to re-employ them subsequently?
- ◆ If employees leave involuntarily, through redundancy,
    - – is an attempt made to help them understand why?
    - – was the process transparent, fair and dignified?
    - – were they given support in planning their future?
    - – does the organization find out how the redundancy process is perceived by whose who leave? by those who stay?

REFERENCES

1. Handy, C. (1994) *The Empty Raincoat*. London: Hutchinson.
2. Noer, D. M. (1993) *Healing the Wounds*. San Francisco: Jossey-Bass.

Part Six

INDIVIDUAL CONTRACTING

Chapter Twenty-One

FINDING OUT

WHAT CAN YOU DO?

Many organizations will have to start re-establishing a psycho-logical contract from scratch. For what they have had with their employees is not a contractual but a coercive employment relation-ship. The same is true for many individuals. For some, the feeling of contract still survived. They felt mightily aggrieved about its inequi-ties, which indicates that they thought that a contract still at least existed. For many, the notion of contract has long gone. Instead of feeling that they are parties to an agreement, they conceive of them-selves as powerless, with only a few options left.

We distinguished three such options: get out, get safe and get even (pp. 83–86). All of these responses fall outside the contracting process:

♦ Getting out means leaving it altogether.
♦ Getting safe means pretending it doesn't exist and hoping it will go away.

♦ Getting even means responding to coercive power by hitting back with whatever personal power you've got left.

Most of us have been attracted to all three responses at some time or other.

These behavioural responses are both consequences of and also feed into the powerlessness and insecurity that employees feel. For example, I may keep my head down below the parapet because I feel powerless; and the longer I stay there the more powerless I feel. This will partly be because I have to justify keeping my head down to myself and to others—"It *must* be dangerous if I'm so insecure"! It's a vicious circle.

However, the same applies in reverse. I'm unlikely to start the contracting process myself— it's too much of a risk. But if I'm encouraged or invited to start it, and if I actually do so, then my feelings will follow suit. I may start to see myself more as a consenting adult than as a frightened fugitive or a vengeful victim. I must be, because I'm acting like one.

We recognize that much of the onus for starting to contract rests with the top management of the organization. After all, in most cases it is they who hold the labour-market power, and hence are taking less of a risk by making the first move. However, we do not underestimate people's capacity for establishing and expressing their wants and offers even when it's apparently dangerous to do so. That's why our last four chapters emphasize what individuals can do to establish and maintain a new psychological contract.

BLOCKS TO DISCOVERY

First, how do *you* find out what you really want, and what you've got to offer? And how do you communicate it?

There are all sorts of reasons why these tasks aren't so easy as they seem at first sight. They range from the obvious to the profoundly personal. More obviously:

1. I may not have realized the possibility that various options were open to me. If I'd known, I might have wanted them.

2. I may not have had the chance to demonstrate in practice what I'm capable of and have to offer.
3. I may not be used to expressing what I want—I might not have had much practice at it lately.
4. I may be inhibited from telling others what I've got to offer ("self-advertisement"!).

Less obviously:

1. My organizational or professional membership has taken up so much of my identity that it prevents me from perceiving what the rest of me needs. I may not even have realized that there *is* a rest of me, and that it *does* need other things!
2. I may not have had the chance to work out for myself what my real value priorities are. The organizational culture, or the sub-culture of my division/business/workgroup, may have provided me with a convenient set of priorities which I have gone along with.
3. I may not realize the relevance of my experience and capabilities to the organization's current and future needs.
4. I may never have had the opportunity to discover what I'm capable of. Or, I demonstrate a variety of capabilities in my non-work activities, but fail to realize that they could carry over.

TOOLS FOR DISCOVERY

So discovery of our value priorities and of our capabilities isn't so easy as at first sight. A personal audit along these lines can go a long way, preferably helped by a friend. If there is the opportunity to use various tools, so much the better. A variety of questionnaire instruments, especially Schein's Career Anchors, can help us to make explicit our career value priorities. Development centres can allow us to try out various work tasks and activities which we can't attempt in the normal course of events. Even annual appraisals can provide some information about our performance (although performance and capabilities are, of course, very distinct).

Another possible source of information is what you are actually used for. For example, experienced middle managers are often used to:

♦ Add reassuring ballast when presenting a proposal to a prospective client.
♦ Mentor younger colleagues, teach them how to get things done and give them career advice.
♦ Act as an organizational lubricant to ensure cross-functional teams work well.
♦ Give advice as to the feasibility of a proposed project in the organizational context.

If people use and value you for these (or other) purposes, what do they think you have to offer? Such evidence as this tends to tell you what others think you're able to do now; your established skills, knowledge and experience. Perhaps unsuspected capabilities can be explored when assignments come up for which volunteers are required. But beware the hospital pass!

WHAT'S GOING ON?

However, we need to do more than discover what we want and can offer. We need to discover organizational information, too. If our organization is as informative as Hewlett-Packard (Chapter Seventeen), then our task is not difficult. But the majority of organizations over the last ten years have nowhere near approached the standards set by HP. Rather, information has largely consisted of a series of directives, informing employees that this or that structural change or management fad will shortly be introduced. So how can we discover what's going on?

A few rules of thumb:

♦ Don't assume the information exists. It is extraordinary what some organizations don't know.
♦ Don't assume that if it does exist, it's available in comprehensible form.

- Don't assume that if it's available in comprehensible form, they'll inform you; you may have to ask for it.
- Don't assume that stated policies have any close relation to practice at grass roots level.

Most are left with the task of gleaning what information we can from "unofficial" sources. These are wider than you think:

- People "in the know" who are often willing to demonstrate how many secrets they are privy to.
- Your own observation of who is in favour, who gets rewarded, promoted and noticed.
- Your knowledge of the business environment—what's going on in your sector?—what sort of jobs are being advertised?—what do others think of your organization?

HOW TO TELL THEM?

Finally, there still remains the task of communicating your wants and offers. While Employee Attitude Surveys allow a general level of communication, their anonymity prevents any individual information being sent by employees. The information pays for its reliability and truthfulness with its loss of particularity.

No, the communication of your own wants and needs is a much more political and tricky process. By way of example, IBM(UK) have recently managed to elicit from their younger employees that what turns them on is:

- teamwork
- recognition and praise
- opportunity to learn
- time with people
- fun at work
- risk-taking
- being involved

What turns them off includes some of the things that we might confidently expect to find in their elders and betters:

- nostalgia
- inflexibility
- workaholism

Now, we all know what happens when young people come out with these things face-to-face! IBM doubtless discovered them anonymously, or from group discussion. The point, of course, is that many communications of wants and expectations challenge the practices, values and assumptions of those with power. Think of the awkward precedents that were predicted if job-sharing were introduced. Think of all the disruption of systems that would supposedly result. How to appreciate the other's anxieties we will discuss in the next chapter. Suffice it to say here that there may be several others whose perspective we have to appreciate. For it may not be one but several different parties who represent "the organization" in the bargaining process:

- our line manager
- management development manager
- business or departmental head
- our patron

Personal career negotiations are indeed tricky!

TIPS, TRICKS AND TIDES: TERRY BATES

Terry Bates is a psychologist, a career counsellor with career management consultants GHN, and many years' experience of working with UK managers. In his work he is often involved in performance coaching of high achievers: those individuals who have been selected for the top, and whose organizations are investing in their development in order to help them get there. Others in his case load have been made redundant, or are under threat. He has therefore wide experience of those who are now core to the organization, and those who wish they still were.

In working with both groups, his advice is that individuals need to have a plan for themselves, a picture of what they would like to have in the next five years in both an ideal world and in a realistic world that acknowledges organizations can no longer make certain guarantees.

How do individuals build up such a picture, particularly those whose careers have previously been managed for them as a reward for their achievements? Terry Bates admits that he was surprised by the evidence of research commissioned by his own company which showed that only 4 per cent of future top managers thought they should have responsibility for managing their careers. Whatever the advice of management writers on self-management, independence from organizational dependence and a focus on self-marketability, it seems that for those who remain the organization's anointed, the possibility of change is still unacknowledged. Bates thinks this rejection of responsibility for their career is a reflection of a number of diverse psychological contracts in operation. For some there is a belief that their abilities earn them the right to favouritism. For others there may be a sense of powerlessness, a belief that since they cannot do anything to change things, they have to rely on the organization and hope it will be OK. There may even be some who are simply blocking an awareness of change, because it is too difficult to accept.

Bates acknowledges that exhorting people to have a plan can seem overwhelming when they have no sense of what to plan for. The key to moving forward is to start collecting information that can both inform individual goals and the process of negotiation.

GHN, like all such career counselling services, places importance on the individual learning more about themselves. A process of such self-evaluation is often a novel experience for people who have taken their evaluation from organizational feedback. Having defined what you are good at by the jobs you are given, gives individuals a skewed picture of their worth and potential. Bates works with individuals to help them discover what they value both in themselves and in their working life. He helps people identify their full range of skills, both by looking closely at what they have achieved and enjoyed, and by considering the feedback they have received: feedback from friends, colleagues, subordinates and networks. In his experience, successful executives are often adept at identifying their functional skills, but often ignore or have failed to develop their communication skills. It hardly needs saying that without having such skills the negotiation process is likely to be difficult. Knowing yourself may well mean working on such areas before starting the process of contracting.

Knowing yourself, however, is insufficient. For successful negotiation, the individual also needs to know the political dimension of the organization. This can help build up a database on who has done what and how. Bates argues that the ways in which outcomes are achieved are never pure. It's as naïve to believe that it is only the "old boys' network" that decides outcomes, as it is to place trust in an appraisal plan being implemented. Individuals need to be intelligence-gathering on how to influence not just from their natural social networks operating at peer level, but from contacts operating at all levels of the organization and across departments. According to Bates, a good check of whether your intelligence network needs extending is to ask yourself when was the last time you sat down and talked to someone you didn't know at lunchtime or at a meeting. The aim is to widen horizons both internally and externally so that new ideas and influences are brought into your intelligence base. Knowing what is happening in competitor organizations, and how they are handling the same people issues, can open up new solutions for putting into the negotiation process.

Alongside building up an individual information base there is a need, according to Bates, to build up a geography of the organization; a picture of where career paths lead (if this is still discernible), of where opportunities are growing and declining, of where power is waxing and waning; knowledge of which special projects are on offer, and how they are viewed, of key task forces and who they report to. The purpose of building up such a topography is to identify where in the organization a preferred form of contract is most likely to find a natural home.

The problem with having worked in organizations and having followed conventional career patterns is that many people have limited ideas on how else it is possible to work. For this reason, Bates encourages contractors to discover more about how things are done differently elsewhere, and not to close their eyes to new developments. Ideas which start out as "off the wall" very rapidly become mainstream, once their organizational advantage becomes clear. He uses the examples of TQM and teleworking as ones which have moved from the fringes to the main stream in a few organizational nanoseconds. If we recognize the rate of change in organizational business practices, why should this be any the less in career management? The good negotiator is one who is ahead of the organization in identifying options and the mutual benefit of those options.

The information-gathering process has to include knowing what HR has in place, and what their power base is. There is little point presenting your case to a Personnel Manager if in reality it is the departmental head who will decide what is acceptable. Indeed, Bates warns against showing your case to HR too early. Individuals need to be aware that HR may not be a "safe house". It cannot be assumed that a testing-out of your half-developed ideas with HR will not become more public knowledge. In an organization looking to shed staff, an exploratory discussion on reducing working hours may fuel a different outcome to the one intended.

Since HR will be involved at some point in the renegotiation of the psychological contract, Bates believes that the discussion should not occur until individuals are clear on their strengths, are confident that their track record gives them bargaining power, and can argue the benefits to the organization of the proposed change. The discussion should also be bounded by a clear sense of what the individual will do if they do not get what they want. Knowing that you will resign if you are not allowed more leeway in how you develop can convey a sense of focus and strength which can influence the other party. Bates talks of the need for psychological robustness, so that if the first suggestion is rejected the employee as negotiator has second and third options, but also knows the point beyond which they will not go.

The final data in the information base is knowing when to act. "The tide in the affairs of men, which taken at the flood leads on to fortune" or, if missed, traps the voyage of life "in shallows and in miseries", is as true for the psychological contractor as it was for Brutus. The smart negotiator will be watching for those times when organizational need and individual want match. It may mean, as Bates warns, that the individual has to bide his or her time. It may also mean that the contracting process has to be broken down into stages, where the eventual goal is kept in sight while the negotiating process edges towards the desired end, at a speed which is manageable for the organization.

INDIVIDUAL INFORMATION CHECKLIST

♦ Do you know what the organization's current business strategy is, and what that means for its staffing policies?

♦ Do you actively seek out information about what is happening in the organization, through official and unofficial routes?

♦ Do you interrogate such information for its human resource implications, or just in business terms?

♦ Do you know where in the organization opportunities are increasing and declining?

♦ Do you know what is happening to other companies in your sector, in both business and human resource terms?

♦ Do you know what human resource policies already exist which could open up options for you?

♦ Do you assume that because policies do not exist, what you would like cannot be possible?

♦ Do you know who has the power base in the organization, to help you achieve what you want?

♦ Do you consciously extend your network within your organization, so that you are gaining information from all directions and at all levels, and not just your peer group?

♦ Do you consciously network outside the organization, so that you can gain a wider picture of what options are being offered to employees elsewhere?

♦ Do you act as an anthropologist, looking at the tribe which is your organization, in order to understand how things get done, and how official policies are interpreted in action?

♦ Do you know the mindset which you are currently bringing to your career, and how this could undermine your approach to the negotiation process?

♦ How powerful/powerless do you currently feel as an entrant into negotiation? If powerless, what information could help you increase your power base?

♦ Do you have a five-year plan for your career, and is it based within an informed picture of the internal and external labour market as it is likely to be in five years time?   *continues*

continued

♦ What sources of official feedback do you have on your skills and how recent was that feedback?

♦ What feedback do you have on your capabilities, based on the ways in which people involve you outside of your official role?

♦ If your career has been managed for you, because of your valued abilities, how sure are you that those skills will hold the same currency in the future?

♦ How well developed are your negotiating skills—do you need help in preparing yourself for a new deals career discussion?

♦ Do you know what your own boundaries are in negotiating a new psychological contract?

Chapter Twenty-Two

GETTING A GOOD DEAL

RULES OF THUMB

There are some well-known rules of thumb about conducting negotiations successfully, and they apply to career negotiations as much as to any others:

♦ Be clear about what you'd like to come out with, but be prepared to compromise.
♦ Have some sort of fall-back position which is the minimum deal you'll accept.
♦ Appreciate the strengths and weaknesses of your own negotiation position, and try to estimate those of the other.
♦ Entertain the possibility of a win–win outcome as well as win–lose or lose–win. And don't forget that lose–lose is not inconceivable!
♦ Recognize the other's perspective. What are likely to be their concerns? Anxiety about precedent? equity? added costs?
♦ Sell the benefits to the other. For example, demonstrate the added value to the organization of what you propose.

♦ Use precedents from inside or outside the organization (especially where these are deemed to be either "best practice" or "common practice").

♦ Go in with a variety of persuasive techniques to hand: evidence to support your case, appeal to equity, business benefit, promises of support ...

♦ Rehearse beforehand various scenarios of how the negotiation could go. Have contingency plans for the two or three most likely.

WHO ARE YOU DEALING WITH?

Clearly, though, there are some particular features of career negotiations which require special attention. In most negotiations, the other negotiator clearly represents the other party, and is empowered to negotiate on its behalf. In career negotiation, this may not be true. Line manager, development manager, function head, business chief executive, patron (if you have one): all may claim to have a stake in your organizational career. The first task, then, is to recognize where each of them is likely to be coming from:

♦ Your line manager may feel he or she has little authority to negotiate and even less knowledge of what can be offered.

♦ The development manager may wish to broaden the range but not the depth of your knowledge.

♦ The function head or business chief executive may want to retain you in your present role because you contribute vitally to his or her business results.

♦ Your patron may need you in another role which more powerfully buttresses his or her own position.

Appreciation of their different perspectives isn't enough, though. The above examples make it clear that some of their interests are incompatible. How can you manage this conflict?

You may need to ask:

♦ What are the current relationships between these individuals?

♦ Which of them has most power to make things happen (or most access to that power)?
♦ Is it possible to get them to join each other in negotiating with you?

COMMITMENTS AND INTENTIONS

Discovering who is the most appropriate representative of the organization is one thing; concluding a successful negotiation with them is something else. For a start, while *you* may be clear both what it is you have to offer and also that you are willing to offer it, they may not have the same confidence. What is the status of their offers? Are they in any position to give undertakings on behalf of top management? Or will business decisions be taken which render any promises impossible to fulfil? Given the likely precarious nature of their offers, the best strategy may well be to look for short-, medium- and longer-term exchanges. Then you can fairly expect the short-term deal to be honoured, but treat the others as intentions rather than promises. So:

1. They promise to consider you (seriously) for the first job that comes up in marketing in the next 3 months; you will immediately start doing some marketing work for a voluntary organization in your "spare time" to give you some more experience.
2. They indicate that they intend to give you an international opportunity when one comes up; you promise not to be choosey where it is, and to go at short notice.
3. They say they are willing to entertain the possibility of a part-time contract for you in the long run; you say you won't push for one until you've completed your present project.

Yet all of these deals assume that the organization is offering you what you want. One of the many pitfalls of negotiation is that we are so pleased to be getting something out of them that we forget to ensure it's something we want and need. It's easy to be seduced by the promise of a broadening of experience into general management when what we really want and need is greater depth in our speciality, for example.

So negotiating's not easy. We might benefit from independent advice and help, if not during the negotiation then before we make up our mind. We certainly need to be clear what the terms of the deal are, and whether they are strong commitments or merely current intentions. In particular, we need to be clear on the legal status of some types of contract, for example part-time contracts.

CONTRACTING WITH KERBY

Alan Kerby is Chairman of executive recruitment company Moxon Dolphin Kerby. He regularly sees executives who have been made redundant after long periods of experience with one organization, and with individual skills that have been largely shaped by that organization. Such individuals do not currently talk of wanting to redefine their psychological contract; their anxiety is to get a new job as quickly as possible. After counselling, they may realize that there are things they expect of an employer, but in the current climate they feel powerless to make those demands.

From Alan Kerby's perspective, there is at present a level playing field only for those people who are in demand, who have quality skills for which there is a labour shortage. But, even for those fortunate few, there are aspects of the contracting process to which they give inadequate attention, and where they fail to recognize their negotiating power.

He believes that most people know insufficient about employment law, and therefore comply with organizational behaviours which in reality are unlawful. He quotes as example companies who will recruit a professional without having them sign a contract before they begin work. Once employed they will be presented with a contract which may place restrictions on their future employment should they leave. For an employee newly in post it is unlikely they will refuse to sign.

Translated into our language of "new deals", there is the equivalent disadvantage of agreeing to join an organization without having a clear idea of what they will offer beyond pay and perks. The employee who fails to check out how far an organization is promising protection, development, flexibility and career management is vulnerable to subsequently discovering a psychological contract where the power overwhelmingly lies with the employer. Since we know that negotiating power is greatest before we commit to an organization, why should this be any less true for the psychological contract?

Alan Kerby also sees executives who take the law at its word. Since in law full employment protection does not come until two years after joining, employees assume this has to be accepted. In reality, such protection could be negotiated at the outset. In psychological terms, assuming that things will not be offered because business conditions are difficult, or the company has had redundancies, could be an equivalent underplaying of the negotiating hand. The lesson has to be "don't assume anything is impossible until directly told so".

Kerby believes that executives grateful for the offer of a job ignore the possibility of another period of unemployment by failing to negotiate a long period of notice. Such a period could both deter an organization from dismissal, or at least give adequate compensation for it. For the psychological contractor, gratitude at being given a job can deflect attention from longer-term needs. Effective negotiation requires holding short-, medium- and long-term perspectives in the head, in which short-term gain is constantly monitored against longer-term objectives.

As part of that longer-term perspective, Kerby believes individuals should be negotiating for what help they will be given should the contract end. Professional career counselling in the event of redundancy should be an explicit part of the employment contract. For our contracting process, individuals should be establishing what sources of help are available when the situation changes, either for the individual or for the organization. This is not only true of redundancy. It may occur with the end of a project, the restructuring of the organization or the end of a clear career route, since all are points at which the individual may want to redefine their own and the organization's perspective.

So how do individuals negotiate from a sense of their own power? For those who are clearly wanted and in demand, the position is clearer. For others, Kerby believes power comes from an inquisitiveness, from knowing what is happening within the organization and in the business environment it is part of; from knowing how power bases are changing in the organization, and who may have the power to give you what you want. It comes also from knowing what you want, and what the organization needs of you. For Kerby, one key is to recognize the difference between your contribution being critical, where organizational dependence will be high, and your contribution being important but non-essential. A second is to recognize when the importance starts to become criticality, for it is at that point that an important power shift occurs. The smart negotiator will grab the tide, and take maximum advantage of that transition before it flows back toward the organization.

The employee as negotiator has to define what benefits they really want out of the process, and be able to prioritize them. This prioritization has to separate the "must haves" from the "would likes". For one person, negotiating longer holiday periods will be a must, for another the crucial issue will be a lengthy period of notice. They must also recognize that expressing those needs gives unspoken messages to the employer. The individual who expresses a need for protection and seeks confirmation of being seen as a long-term investment is also signalling a sense of vulnerability that the organization may subsequently use to withhold other offers. The individual who signals a need for freedom and autonomy will have set in motion a different arena for future negotiations.

Kerby believes that seeking long-term assurances is probably a fruitless negotiation aim, and that even where security needs are high, a more realistic agenda is to negotiate for the best possible deal in moving towards what is probable. A recognition of what the organization is likely to offer, and negotiating within those boundaries, is more likely to achieve an acceptable compromise than attempting to control the outcome from a purely personal agenda. A person who knows that sudden redundancy would be personally traumatic because "what next" is a frightening void could look to negotiate a gradual withdrawal where, over an agreed time, involvement is reduced from full-time to part-time to exit.

In talking of such a shift, Kerby acknowledges that such negotiations are more likely to take place in small organizations where the organization will flex its offerings where it sees a direct benefit. In his own company, teleworking is accepted for a female employee who was previously commuting 5 hours a day. The negotiation process was based on the organization's awareness that she was likely to leave and was unlikely to relocate nearer to the office, that she had valued skills and that home working would give her more hours a day to contribute. Her negotiation was based on her offering of extensive client knowledge, and cost reductions. The negotiation process was one of building a bridge where the organization's willingness to flex its requirements was buttressed by an awareness that in flexing they were buying her longer-term loyalty.

KEEPING TIME WITH KIT SCOTT BROWN

Kit Scott Brown is the Chief Executive of InterExec, a company which is unique in the UK in offering both outplacement and inplacement. The concept of outplacement is widely understood, and is one business sector that has flourished in the 1990s. Inplacement, however, is less well known. It is the use of professionals to help people who are in work find their next job. For Kit Scott Brown, such a service has an unarguable logic. Given that most people learn job search skills through trial and error, and in ways which are time-intensive, why not offer a service where professionals carry out that work for you? The dual perspectives of dealing with those who have seen their career path fractured by redundancy, and of working with those who, though employed, want something different, give him a wide perspective on the negotiation process.

At the present time he sees redundant executives who are experiencing "feelings of castration". They are fearful of both the present and the future. Their emotional response is to seek to avoid being made unemployed ever again. Does this mean they look to protect themselves against ever being organizationally dependent through accepting the concept of career self-management? Not according to Scott Brown. Their aim when they seek his help is to find a new job that will last until they retire. Given that his average client is aged 45, and the majority still see retirement as 20 years ahead, it is an expectation that is unlikely to be met.

Kit Scott Brown sees it as his job to help clients understand the reality of what their future will be, and to help them plan towards it. From his perspective the individual/organizational time frame should now be three to five years, with an expectation that retirement is more likely to occur in their 50s than their 60s. While these may seem like harsh truths to present to an executive already bruised by redundancy, Kit Scott Brown sees negotiating strengths coming from their acceptance.

Recognition that retirement may well occur at 50 draws into focus the importance of financial planning. It highlights the reality of the sort of package the executive needs to be negotiating for. If a second career opens up after 50, or another organizational job appears, they become bonuses, not necessities. Scott Brown is regularly astonished how little thought able executives have given to financially planning for the most likely career outcome. From our perspective of the psychological contract, the individual who is able to assess coolly what is the most likely offer the organization will make, rather than basing their plans on what they would ideally like, begins to build up a new negotiating position. They are able to make additional financial demands to compensate for the inability of the organization to give their most preferred option. Scott Brown regrets the fact that organizations are still reluctant to open about the reality of job timescales. In avoiding talk of the expected time span, they are colluding with the employee who seeks, because of recent experience, to find reassurance in what is not said. Matching time dimensions is a key aspect of negotiating a satisfactory new deal.

Is it possible to make such a deal in the present climate? Scott Brown thinks it is. He believes that a shift away from an expectation of long-term organizational security, to clear contracting where individuals understand that they are there to do a specific job that is expected to end at a defined date, has benefits to both parties. For the individual, there is an incentive to perform at their best in order that their marketability is high at the point of separation. From the organization's perspective, investment in training employees becomes an offer to ensure meeting present performance needs and building future employability. Even more radically, Scott Brown sees a time contract as opening up the possibility of bonuses for work completed ahead of schedule. The contracting process could then include an explicit statement as to payments to be made at the point of separation when targets have been exceeded. He sees a psychological difference between a redundancy payment which is viewed by the employee as compensation for the breaking of the old deal, and a bonus payment in recognition of leaving the organization as a success.

In terms of the psychological contract, Scott Brown's enthusiasm for time contracting brings into focus the individual's need to have defined goals within which a particular time contract fits, so that there is an incentive for entry and exit, not entry and linger. He quotes the example of a manager in the wine trade, whose aim of running his own chain of wine stores rested on his being able to raise £500 000. Since this was an impossible short-term goal, he explicitly sought out wine businesses who were in need of turn-around management help. His negotiation position was to contract for a period of time in which he guaranteed to achieve identified goals, with the promise of a bonus if they were achieved ahead of time. Through a number of such appointments he was able to acquire the £500 000 he needed to establish his own business. Our goals may be less ambitious, but the principle within which he worked holds true. Since organizations do not want to be limited by unbounded time commitments, this gives employees the possibility of identifying new win–win options.

There is an additional aspect of time, which Scott Brown believes organizations and individuals have yet to acknowledge—that of career time. He argues that if individuals and organizations openly accepted that on average, in the future, we may not work for 25 per cent of our expected work life span, then individuals would develop financial and social plans for that free time. It would clearly focus thoughts more stringently on financial negotiations, and open up greater honesty on both sides. In accepting that a career may more often follow that of an actor (often resting) than an accountant (never resting), different types of dialogue become possible, with less judging of unconventional career patterns. Scott Brown's analysis highlights the need in future contracting for both sides to focus ahead, rather than continuing to look in the rearview mirror as the point of reference. The deals he describes have less threat to those now entering the labour market, but are still unpalatable to those who have defined themselves as creatures of the organization.

INDIVIDUAL NEGOTIATION CHECKLIST

♦ When moving into a new organization, or moving into a new job, do you consider the psychological contract you are seeking, as well as the benefits package?

♦ Have you established what you'd like, based on a full assessment of what's possible, or based on what is already on offer?

♦ Are you clear on what is already legitimated by policy agreement, even if examples of take-up are difficult to find?

♦ Are you clear on your employment rights? If you are thinking of working more flexibly, you need to be clear on the financial and legal implications of your choice.

♦ Are you fully informed on what your financial needs are, should you retire before statutory retirement age?

♦ What time span are you operating to when looking to negotiate with the organization? How realistic is that, given the evidence of what you see happening to others?

♦ What negotiating options are open to you if you define the length of time you expect the contract to last, and what you want it to lead towards?

♦ Within the negotiation process, can you break down your needs into short- and medium-term goals?

♦ Are you clear about which points are negotiable and which are not?

♦ Do you know how critical your skills are to the organization's ability to achieve its aims? Is this changing, to your or the organization's advantage?

♦ Looked at from the organization's perspective, what are the strengths and weaknesses of your negotiating position? Which strengths have most leverage to overcome the blockages presented by your weaknesses?

♦ Do you know what might legitimately stop the organization from agreeing to your request? If it is not possible, does that knowledge open up alternative options that could still be acceptable?

continues

177

continued

♦ Have you rehearsed selling your case in terms that focus on the business benefits, rather than the personal benefits?

♦ What sources of help are available to support you in the negotiation process, e.g. are you a member of a learning group? Does your trade union or staff association have an interest? Do you have a mentor?

♦ Do you know with whom you should be negotiating, i.e. who has the power to give you what you want?

♦ Do you know what is your preferred influencing style? Are you likely to use facts, carrots or sticks, or emotional appeals to shared interests? How well does your style match with that of the person/people you need to influence? Do you need to work on developing your range of influencing styles?

♦ Do you have a timescale for achieving your new contract, broken down into short- and medium-term goals?

Chapter Twenty-Three

KEEPING AN EYE

Now that we've made a deal, how do we check up that it's being kept? *They* check up on *my* performance regularly—monthly budget targets, quarterly performance reviews, annual appraisals. Why shouldn't *I* appraise *them*? After all, it's a two-sided bargain, so why should only one of the parties be checked up on?

We first need to address the overall balance of the deal. Have they fulfilled their promised offers, or are those promises fading into oblivion?

♦ Will I *ever* get that additional support colleague they said they'd recruit, or will it be judged politically impossible in the light of redundancies elsewhere in the organization?
♦ Will I be given the chance of working abroad before I start a family, or has that promise, too, been quietly shelved?
♦ Are they going to talk with me about a way to phase me gradually into retirement through some consultancy, or have they forgotten they ever said they would?

In sum, are they keeping their promises?

But that's not the only area we have to monitor. Perhaps they are offering what they said they'd *offer*, but at the same time stealthily adding more items to their *wants* list.

♦ A colleague has been made redundant, perhaps, and a third of her job seems to have ended up on your plate.
♦ You have acquired management of a key account—a mark of trust and recognition; but it means a lot of extra travel and out-of-hours entertaining.
♦ Your resources remain the same, but your profitability targets increase every year.

So they may fail to come up with their offers, or they may unilaterally add to their wants. Either way, the balance of the original deal has been disturbed—inequity intrudes. What to do? Shall I readjust the balance surreptitiously by putting less effort in? Draw their attention to it explicitly? Seek to reverse the change and get back to the original deal? Decide the clock can't be put back and so try to negotiate a new deal? Give up and get out? Answers in the next chapter!

The importance of monitoring the state of the deal from our own perspective cannot be overemphasized. If we fail to do so, we may find ourselves shocked and outraged by a particular experience which strikes us as a flagrant violation. Yet if we had been checking, we would have noticed a series of tell-tale signs that all was not well. There are always *some* indications that they are going to take half your staff away or double your targets or label you "plateaued". And when shocked and outraged, we may do something which doesn't serve our best interests in the long run.

Even from our own perspective, though, there are still two sides to the deal—their wants and offers *and* ours. Do we monitor what we ourselves are offering? Are we unaware:

♦ That we are working more hours per week than last year?
♦ That our technical skills are getting a bit rusty?
♦ That our overall commitment to the organization has decreased in line with an ever-increasing and debilitating cynicism?
♦ That our value has increased because there is now a shortage in the labour market of our skills?

If we're not, we should be.

Perhaps we are not delivering our side of the bargain because we weren't fully committed to the deal when it was made. Perhaps it was forced upon us, or perhaps we didn't fully understand the implications.

And what about changes in what we want? This isn't a matter of monitoring the deal itself. It's rather our own lives and the business situation that we should be keeping an eye on. First, ourselves; or rather, our selves. For while the changes in our roles are easy for us to spot, changed value priorities and identities may not be so clearly visible. We are only too aware, for example, of the onset of parent-hood, or of when we start to become protectors of our own parents. We come to appreciate the implications of these new roles on what we want from work: more security as a parent, perhaps, and clear weekends as a carer. But are we aware of the more gradual and subtle changes in our values and identities? Have we, for example, asked ourselves recently what single thing about our career we could not now give up? Or whether there are major aspects of our organiza-tion's activities which now violate our current value priorities? Perhaps we realize that without a technical/functional component, our work loses its meaning for us and we lose part of our profes-sional identity in the process. Or perhaps greater emphasis on the bottom line has compromised our recently rediscovered need to do good quality work of which we can be proud.

Finally, are we monitoring some of the general changes in the organization? Are we looking at the cultural artefacts which give us clues about changing values and assumptions? Who, for example, gets promoted nowadays? Which achievements are selected for praise and recognition? What new systems are being put in? What management fad is currently being embraced? Which projects is the organization getting involved in? And, looking more externally, how is the organization performing in its sector? What are the perceptions of the business press regarding our organization's performance? What general sectoral trends are there (for example, a greater em-phasis on marketing)?

In the last analysis, though, the crunch question really is: how do I feel on Sunday evening about going to work on Monday morning? Allowing for start-of-the-week blues, if I nevertheless regularly feel dread at the prospect; if I know I'm going to disagree with most of what's said and done; if I feel angry at the inequity, or helpless in the face of the hopelessness of it all, then things have to change or I have to get out. One way or another, I need a new deal.

The importance of self monitoring is highlighted in this account of the issues that get brought to a career counselling service by individuals who have failed for too long to check their personal litmus paper.

TAKING THE PULSE: VALERIE HOPKINS

Valerie Hopkins is founder of Humanitas, a consultancy which describes itself as concerned with human needs. Their aim is to provide support to organizations and individuals as they experience change. It is a claim which Valerie Hopkins's own life experience can support. Trained as an accountant, she is a city investment analyst turned trained counsellor, who has a perspective both on how individuals are impacted by change and why organizations demand change. She is therefore in a strong position to look at the present state of the psychological contract, and to advise employers and employees on where they need to take a greater responsibility.

The companies she is working with, many of them major City players, are starting to look at the expectations they have of key employees, and are acknowledging that placing such high demands earns them the right to organizational support. The people she sees are perceived as outstanding performers but ones who are out of step with the behaviours the organization expects.

She quotes the example of a 55-year-old man, recognized as the company's highest income earner, but perceived by others as impossible to work with. The prevailing HR response would be to impose a generous early retirement package. Instead, he was offered counselling to work on those behaviours which were causing difficulties. During counselling, he was able to acknowledge the frustration, isolation and fear of being on the scrap heap, that he brought with him to work each day. His daily motivation was avoiding redundancy by keeping profits up. The consequences this had for others he had no means of handling. Through exposing his fears he has been able to go back into work and ask colleagues for feedback, so that when he is going "off the rails" he can monitor and change his actions. He has come to share Hopkins's belief that even a small individual change will impact on how the organizational system deals with him. His goal now is to find a way of working towards retirement in which he will have a sense of personal control. The emotions he takes to that process are far different from those he would have taken to involuntary retirement.

What counselling is offering such individuals is an opportunity to monitor their satisfaction with how their working life is, to evaluate its appropriateness for their own wellbeing and to find new ways of behaving which link with organizational needs. Because of their value to the organization, the company is creating the conditions for monitoring and re-evaluation that most employees have to discover for themselves.

The one area of employee welfare in which organizations have taken a declared interest in recent years has been stress management. Much of that interest has focused on getting individuals to manage their own stress. Discover what stress does to you physically and mentally, and develop a repertoire of positive techniques for coping with an overload of demand and an undersupply of control. Nowhere in the 1980s agenda has there been a questioning of the reasons for that over-demand, and of the organization's responsibility for making systems change to correct it.

Hopkins is working with organizations who are now taking a different approach to stress management, by acknowledging that organizational demands are damaging to individuals and their families, and that both parties have a responsibility. She is currently involved in a new initiative by a major UK finance company to ensure its future senior managers are not damaged by the expectations placed on them. The company offer is not to reduce demand, but to help individuals develop coping strategies through monitoring themselves and their reactions more closely. Hopkins sees highly skilled individuals who are coping with task expectations, but rarely consider that they could manage their lives more healthily. She is able to help them develop positive strategies by allowing them to evaluate their feelings about their current job, the sources of pressure, their coping tactics, their interpretation of events around them and their general repertoire of behaviours. While the work is starting with the personal, one outcome will be aggregate feedback to the organization on what it is doing which is causing stress to its future leaders. The key differentiator in this approach to stress management is that the contract has a feedback mechanism back into organizational systems.

While this chapter is concerned with individual monitoring of satisfaction with the psychological contract, the fact that such services as Humanitas exist for key core workers is a recognition that monitoring is a behaviour often missing from an individual's repertoire until a crisis occurs. In Valerie Hopkins's work it is the organization which is bringing to individuals' attention that they are failing in some way to fully deliver their part of the deal: that part which is to do with how skills are delivered. What the counselling process can do is to unearth the reasons for those behaviours. Hopkins discovers that beneath "difficult" employees are often depressed individuals with low self-esteem, paralysed by a sense of personal impotence. They have silently monitored their situation, come to the conclusion there is nothing to be done, and accepted a minimum goal of survival. With help, they come to believe they do have agency, and that rather than judging themselves against organizational culture, they can look at organizational culture against their needs. While many initially hope for a miracle cure, they come to realize that the perfect job may not be there, but that once they find their own strength they can say "This is who I am, how do I need to change for you?" When they acknowledge their own ability to change, they often find that the organization will shift also.

But if counselling isn't available, what can individuals and organizations do to help the monitoring process? Valerie Hopkins believes that the ground rules have to be established at the start of employment, so that the agenda becomes: What will the individual offer, and how will the organization show that the individual is valued? Whatever measure of valuing the organization declares, whether that is training and development, financial advancement, high-profile assignments or promotion, can then be monitored by the individual. If the contract is met, even if the employment ends, the individual and the organization can part on good terms. Beyond open contracting, Hopkins argues that individuals need to be helped to monitor the impact of personal changes on themselves. One organizational offering that would assist self-monitoring would be to help employees understand that reactions to change are impacted by past experiences and present life stage. Helping people to monitor themselves, and encouraging a climate in which individual change is matched by organizational response, would reduce the unspoken resentments and bruised confidence of many who see their present psychological contract as fixed.

INDIVIDUAL MONITORING CHECKLIST

♦ Does your monitoring of the organization and its competitors extend to monitoring the impact of changes on yourself?

♦ If you recognize changes in yourself in response to business changes, are you happy with the behaviours you are using in order to justify your place at work?

♦ Are you monitoring the effect on your family of the current deal? Are they giving you messages that it's time for change?

♦ Do you monitor the impact your behaviours have on others and their response to you? If relationships at work are less comfortable than they once were, is this affecting your ability to achieve work objectives?

♦ Do you believe there is anything you can do to bring about change? Or are you fatalistic about the possibility of an individual being able to change themselves, or their response to their situation?

♦ How much control over your situation do you feel yourself to have? A sense of low control, high demands, low organizational support and working with uncertainty add up to a rich recipe for stress.

♦ Do you monitor how much support the organization gives you, and whether that is sufficient for you to be able to perform at your best? What else could they do that would help your performance?

♦ Are you feeling stressed? Or do you even recognize the signs of stress in yourself? Recognizing one's own stress, and the personal costs, is a good motivator for change.   *continues*

continued

♦ Do you monitor the balance between your work and home life? Has it changed in recent years, and what have been the consequences for you?

♦ Do you monitor changes in your life roles? Is the mixture of roles, e.g. parent, partner, carer, community member, student—changing, and if so what are the implications for you and your role of worker?

♦ Do you monitor the external environment, so that your specific experiences can be put into a wider social and economic context?

♦ Do you take stock of your responses to work, even when you are not operating in crisis management mode? Internal change can occur independent of organizational change.

♦ Do you monitor yourself and the environment for evidence of changes which are positive as well as negative?

♦ Do you monitor yourself against what you believe you can be, rather than against how you seem to need to be in order to survive in your organization?

♦ What are the ways in which your organization signals value? Are you a recipient of this recognition? If you are not is it because you hold different values?

♦ Do you know what you are valued for, and are they things which you value in yourself?

Chapter Twenty-Four

GET A NEW DEAL OR GET OUT

You've decided things can't go on as they are. What can you do about it? For many, the first answer that comes into their head is: *nothing*. They are trapped, they feel: mortgages need paying, children and parents need supporting, pensions need securing. Anyway, it's hard to give up a lifestyle we've come to feel comfortable in. We may have less and less opportunity to enjoy it, but we feel we can't surrender it.

We may not even have the choice. We may be made redundant next week. Renegotiation of the deal may be forced on us as the only way of avoiding redundancy; perhaps a part-time lifestyle contract may be offered, or a fixed-term contract. These are usually offers we cannot refuse. Coercion, not contracting, is the order of the day. The outcome is certainly in the organization's interests, but it may not be what we want for ourselves.

Renegotiation can be proactive, though. We can take the initiative ourselves. We may have spotted that our own offers could change to take account of the organization's changing wants: a win–win outcome. We may have developed new skills specifically to enable us to meet these new organizational requirements. Yet we need, perhaps, to ask whether familiarity with the organization and attachment to colleagues and ways of working may blind us to the possibility of a better deal elsewhere. After all, the skills we have newly developed may merely keep us in a job with our present employers; they may get us a better one with others.

The converse, of course, is equally seductive. A headhunter offers us another position with a much better package than we receive at present. Or a job advertisement raises hopes that the grass will be greener. Yet neither familiarity nor benefits package should dominate our decision whether to renegotiate or leave. We should beware of seeing the headhunter as a rescuing knight helping us out of our slough of despond; rescue from the miry swamp may only lead to being dumped in the Sahara. The headhunter may put a far higher price on their financial deal with the employer, than they do on satisfying your personal needs. If employability is our major concern, then the most important question has to be this: will renegotiation with my present employer or a move to a new one better enhance my employability?

There's one thing we should remember about the renegotiation option, however. It is that the new deal we conclude with our company certainly won't be a relational one. Most renegotiations now involve the move from a relational to a transactional deal. Both parties now have an interest in being more specific about what is being exchanged for what; employees, in particular, will not intend going the extra mile only to risk getting kicked in the teeth in return.

So, we may not even try renegotiation. Or, if we do, we may fail. How do we, then, manage exit to our advantage? It's terribly easy for exit to be an ill-tempered and churlish episode. How can they explain satisfactorily to themselves that someone should choose to leave their splendid organization? He wasn't really up to the job, they say; or, she never really settled in and took the culture on board. We, too, can make parting something other than such sweet sorrow. Demob-happy, we tell a few hometruths to the wrong people, spend more time preparing for our new job than completing our present one, and try to take a quiverful of clients with us. Revenge may be sweet, but it's also dangerous.

Yet, just as KPMG derive benefit from their leavers (see pp. 148–151), so we can exit both gracefully and profitably. Our new employer may be a potential client of our present one, or a potential supplier. If it is a competitor, the situation is trickier. We may feel able to assure our present employer that there are some things we would treat as confidential—would they tell us what they wish not to be revealed?

Our present employer is also a potential source of work for the future. If we are going out on our own, or joining a smaller supplier, then contracts may be in the offing. It is therefore vital that we maintain goodwill, since we may be a supplier, a consultant or even possibly an employee again. We cannot, for example, afford ourselves the luxury of using the exit interview as a dumping ground for any anger and frustration we may feel.

But all this assumes that we've got somewhere to go. The danger, of course, is that we leap at the first opportunity that's offered on the assumption that we're not likely to get too many more. Yet this presupposes we have to wait for opportunities to present themselves. Here again, proactivity is the order of the day. Having made the decision in principle to exit, we keep quiet about it. We work out what our own wants and offers are and what we'd hope for by way of return. Then we think carefully who in our network is likely to know of a potential opportunity and ask them, in confidence, to keep their ears and eyes open on our behalf, giving them an idea of the sort of deal we're looking for.

Simultaneously, we scan advertisements and discover the sort of organization that may offer us what we want. The *Personnel Yearbook* will give us the right Personnel person to contact, or we may be able to deal with someone in our own functional area. We need to make the first approach, preferably by 'phone, and have a CV ready to send. This will be variable to suit each organization but will probably retain the same basic structure. It should state, primarily, what you have to offer in the light of what you have discovered about what they need.

How to choose whether or not to accept an offer, or which to accept, given several? A useful strategy is to look at the nature of your deal at exit from your present organization:

- What have *you* got to offer that they aren't accepting?
- What do *you* need that they cannot/will not offer?
- What are *they* offering that you don't want?
- What do *they* want that you cannot/will not offer?

The points at which you found this deal unsatisfactory are those to pay particular attention to when seeking to make a new one.

But above all, the changed context of the employment relationship means you will be looking to make new sorts of deal. In the midst of a revolution, it's those fast on their feet who survive. In Mike Crowther's account of renegotiation, we see that quickness of foot does not necessarily mean speeding out through the door. For him, negotiating for autonomy made staying a more attractive option than exiting.

A NEW DEAL ON TIME: MIKE CROWTHER

Mike Crowther is a good role model for those who are looking to renegotiate. He is a professional in early middle age, who at a time when others around him are seeing the only option as giving more and more in order to justify their employment, has negotiated a reduced time commitment to work.

His desire for change came from a number of recognitions. Some years ago he changed employer. Previously he had seen himself, and been used, as a strategic core employee. He had been involved in decision-making on HR issues, he had been trusted with information, and was confident that he always knew what was happening. He was frequently consulted by more senior managers because they recognized the depth of his experience. He knew his voice had a right to be heard, even if that voice was not always agreed with.

He quickly realized in his new employment that he was marginalized within the core. He felt excluded not just from decision-making, but from the information that informed decision-making. The contribution he was being asked to make was more limited than what he believed he could contribute. Equally importantly, the way in which he was expected to contribute rancoured. A tightening of the business environment reinforced a "tell" style of management, which was then compounded by the introduction of new systems designed to exercise a tighter control over his work. These changes highlighted to Mike the expectations he had of an employer: that he should be allowed to contribute all that he was able, and that he should be given autonomy in how he achieved his ends. He came to realize that when he worked long hours on a project, he expected to have the leeway of taking some recovery time. That leeway was no longer on offer.

His first reaction was to look elsewhere; to find an environment that would place fewer controls on his use of time. For such a freedom he was prepared to accept a drop in his future salary. As job opportunities were few, another strategy emerged: to negotiate with his employer for more time. He came to realize that the stress symptoms he was experiencing were not the result of disliking his job; rather, they were the result of long hours which left him little time to relax even when not working. What Mike was looking for was time to be him; time to spend with his family, to do things by himself that he enjoyed, to read and think.

When he first raised the idea with Personnel, it was rejected. A year on he asked if his package would be different if he was a reduced-hour worker, and this time the question caught the interest of Personnel. They asked him to tell them more about his ideas. The idea was now of interest because it raised the possibility of reducing costs at a time when reaching business targets was proving difficult.

Encouraged, Mike put together a paper identifying what was in it for the organization, if he should reduce his hours. He highlighted how in a seasonal business he could be used when demand was high; he argued that a less stressed employee would be a better contributor, and he convinced them that he was not going to use time away to set up in competition.

His success in convincing the organization was not due to his efforts alone. Personnel offered to present his case to management anonymously, so that if it was rejected there would be no "come back" on his future career. They also acted as a guide as to when the case should be presented. With a closer involvement in the business, they were able to judge when the time was ripe to push the proposal.

The outcome was not as originally defined in the paper. Mike gave more on some areas, but then was able to win concessions on others. Importantly, he negotiated that the arrangement was reversible, so that at any time in the future either side could ask that he return as a full-time core worker, provided that a period of notice was given. He has also ensured that the arrangement is reviewed so that if working satisfactorily, it is positively renewed. Mike has taken a risk, but that risk has been reinforced by the enthusiasm with which colleagues have responded to his new contract. It has shown him that his contract expectations are ones which are shared by others, even if they do not have the confidence or personal circumstances to make the change.

Having gone through the process, Mike believes he has learned a number of lessons for future contractors:

1. The key to acceptance may well lie in raising the issue when business conditions demand more flexible thinking. It is therefore important to be monitoring the business climate, so that even if an idea is initially rejected, the opportunity for a second chance is not missed.

2. The sales pitch has to be in terms of what the organization is going to gain from the change, rather than focusing on the benefits to the individual.

3. It is important to develop a link with the organizational system. It need not be Personnel, but it has to be with someone who understands how things are done, and can act as your representative.

4. The proposed contract should be developed in concert with someone who can represent the organization's point of view, and can help you shape your proposal.

5. Before making your offer, consult with Personnel on the legal implications. More flexible ways of working can have profound impacts on employment protection and pension entitlement unless they are well planned.

INDIVIDUAL RENEGOTIATION CHECKLIST

♦ Are you looking to renegotiate or exit because of strong emotional feelings about your situation? Are you feeling angry, betrayed, unfairly treated? Before doing anything, you need to cool down and assess what it is that is making you angry. Negotiations fuelled by emotion alone are unlikely to allow you to feel in control of the process.

♦ What elements are there in your present work which, if altered, could permit a satisfying employment relationship? Exiting could result in a less satisfactory outcome than looking to renegotiate the present deal.

♦ What signals are there in the organization that now is a good or bad time to be looking to renegotiate? The timing of your request can be crucial to its success.

♦ Are you sure that you have banked sufficient personal value in terms of your skills and past contribution to give you a strong personal power base for renegotiation? If your personal account is underfunded, the organization will have little investment in entering the renegotiation process.

♦ Have you identified those areas of performance delivery which would add most to your personal power base when renegotiating? How much are you prepared to risk? There is no point using threats of exiting if your needs are not met, unless you are prepared to follow through.

♦ Are there skills and experiences which you have used in your past which could be better used in the present? Offering to use those skills could open up ways of reframing your job, that could meet your own and the organization's needs. Don't forget your past experience as part of your negotiation offerings.

♦ Have you clarified in your mind what your expectations and offers are? Assertive renegotiation can only come from clarity as to the ends you are seeking. That doesn't mean they will be achieved in full. However, starting negotiations from a position of unease without having an identified goal will leave you open to direct rejection or manipulation.

continues

continued

◆ Have you looked at the external labour market in order to assess whether the deal you are wanting is more easily achievable in a new setting or through working within the one you know?

◆ Have you a trusted colleague with whom you can try out your ideas and receive feedback on how to present them effectively?

◆ Have you thought what next? Are you intending the renegotiation to be the beginning of a separation process, or could you envisage the new arrangement being reversed? You need to be clear, so that you can build in safeguards to protect your future options.

POSTSCRIPT

Since we finished writing this book, two significant events have occurred in the UK. First, Secretary of State for Employment, Michael Portillo, has been forced by a judgment of the House of Lords to accept that part-time employees have the same rights as full-timers regarding unfair dismissal and redundancy payments (Crown vs Secretary of State for Employment *ex parte* Equal Opportunities Commission, 1994, IRLR 176). Nevertheless, other rights for part-timers embodied in the EU directive on this topic remain to be fully implemented.

Second, a landmark legal judgment has been made by the High Court (Walker vs Northumberland County Council). Mr Walker, a social worker, successfully sued his employer for damages, the current estimate of which is £200 000. The grounds for the judgment and the award were that the Council had failed to provide due care in the way in which Mr Walker was managed. The judgment clearly implied that the employer was responsible for the stress and subsequent illness which the employee suffered. While this case clearly has implications for the nature of the employment relationship, too much weight cannot be placed upon it as case law. This is because Mr Walker's plight was extreme; it was only after his second nervous breakdown that the employer's culpability was judged to be proven.

These cases are straws in the wind, signalling the first signs of a dawning realization in the UK that the labour marked and the employment relationship cannot be considered as a free and unregulated market. Legislation (particularly legislation with financial teeth) focuses top management's mind wonderfully. But the landmark cases we have cited are not the only signs of a sea change. The Prime Minister and the Confederation of British Industry have both publicly argued against the current high level of directors' remuneration and benefits. The implication is that they believe there are equity considerations over and above the bare market rate. Parliament and media have expressed grave concern about events in the recently-privatized utilities, where the contrast between the increases in top managements' salaries post-privatization and the pay-offs to newly-redundant staff is a gross offence.

Thus, even though the labout market power is still, generally speaking, with the buyer, fundamental questions are beginning to be asked. The overblown rhetoric of the Human Resource ideology and the management fads is being punctured. Gradually, even those who introduced and promoted the rhetoric are becoming aware that few believe it any more. Reality is intruding at last. People are ceasing to mouth slogans.

Of course, recognition of reality is only the first step. But the fact that we found four organizations for our case studies, and that now we could find several others, suggests more. It suggests that the top management of some organizations is starting to treat its managers, professionals and workforce as partners with whom they have a contract. They are treating them with dignity as adult human beings. Only if we all define ourselves as contractors rather than resource managers or victims will we regain the self-esteem to take risks and to think innovatively. And only then will we and our organizations stay in business.

INDEX